WELCOME TO
THE CLASSIC
JOE
WICKS
COLLECTION

This collection brings together two of my favourite books
– the one that started it all, *Lean in 15: The Shift Plan*,
and my gorgeous hardback, *Joe's 30-Minute Meals*.
These books are packed with banging recipes that taste
incredible and are really quick and easy to make. I hope
you enjoy cooking and eating them as much as I do!

Joe

First published 2015 by Bluebird
This omnibus edition first published 2019 by Bluebird
an imprint of Pan Macmillan
The Smithson, 6 Briset Street, London EC1M 5NR
Associated companies throughout the world
www.panmacmillan.com

ISBN 978-1-5290-3634-3

Visit www.panmacmillan.com to read more about all our books and to buy them. You will
also find features, author interviews and news of any author events, and you can sign up

Bluebird publish inspirational lifestyle books, bringing you the
very latest in diet, self-help and popular psychology, as well as
parenting, career and business, and memoir.

We make books for life in every sense: life-enhancing but also
lasting; the ones you will turn to again and again for inspiration.

For 10 extra Lean in 15 recipes and to hear more about
Bluebird visit www.beachleanin15.com

CONTENTS

A LITTLE BIT ABOUT ME

//

When I posted my first ever #Leanin15 video on Instagram in early 2014, I never imagined it would lead to me writing this book. It all started as a bit of fun in my kitchen, with the idea of sharing simple recipes to help people get lean.

All of the meals were ready in 15 minutes, and the videos were only 15 seconds long . . . hence the hashtag #Leanin15. To begin with, no one was watching my videos, and my neighbours thought I was mad. They often heard me singing or shouting, 'Bosh, that's Lean in 15' and 'Oooh, midget trees' (that's what I call broccoli, by the way!).

Some of my friends thought it was stupid, and said I should get back to doing personal training and running my boot camps – that's what I had been happily doing for the past 5 years. But I was having fun, so I just carried on anyway, often posting up to 3 videos a day. It took a lot of time and energy to stop and film everything I cooked, but I saw every meal as an opportunity to share a new recipe, and this was my motivation to keep going.

> **I saw every meal as an opportunity to share a new recipe**

To my surprise, within a few months, hundreds of thousands of people all over the world were following along, making my recipes at home and sharing them online. I think the speed and simplicity of my meals, along with the fact that I was clearly enjoying myself, inspired so many people to get involved.

I'm completely self-taught when it comes to cooking, so I never over-complicate things. I use foods that anyone can find in their local supermarket and this makes Lean in 15 accessible to everyone and perfect for busy people.

My approach is also about making small lifestyle changes rather than following a strict regime. I often post photos of myself eating out in restaurants and enjoying treats. I do love a chocolate fondant – guilty as charged!

I think people respond well to me, because I don't eat perfectly all the time, and I never pretend that I do. In fact, my diet used to be pretty shocking. I've always trained hard, but I didn't really take my nutrition seriously. Like most busy people, I was lazy when it came to cooking and used lack of time as an excuse. I often ate cereal, sandwiches on the go and ready meals. This left me feeling tired, but I just accepted it as normal. I drank fizzy drinks and snacked on chocolate bars in between personal training clients. During this time, my body didn't change much and I could never get lean. Eventually, I discovered that no matter how hard I trained, I couldn't out-train a poor diet.

It was only when I really started to study nutrition after university that I realized just how important real food was for my energy levels and making changes in my body. The more I understood, the more I started to transform my own body. With this new knowledge and understanding of nutrition, I was able to get lean and stay lean. I then started to apply my knowledge with my clients, and it was remarkable how quickly their bodies would respond. Helping clients get fast transformations meant I soon got fully booked as a personal trainer. But, even with two busy

> **My approach is also about making small lifestyle changes rather than a strict regime**

6

boot camps, I could only ever work with about 100 people each week. This wasn't enough for me. I wanted to help more people reach their goals, so I started putting more energy into my social media. With Twitter, Facebook, YouTube and Instagram, I was able to reach thousands of people at once by sharing content online – video recipes, workouts and blogs. As my social media following grew, I started to realize just how shocking the diet industry really was. Every day I would receive messages from people on all sorts of depressing low-calorie crash diets, and it soon became apparent just how much wrong information people were being given – and how far they were willing to go to lose weight. Regimes of training for 2 hours a day and eating fewer than 1000 kcal were way too common, and it upset me that people were living this way, always trying to find a shortcut and never getting the results they wanted. Very unhappy people were being held prisoner to diets that would never give them the lean body they wanted. I believe such crash diets are a contributory factor to so many of the eating disorders and body image issues we face today. People have become convinced that the only way to lose body fat is to drastically cut calories to create a huge energy deficit – but this only leads to yo-yo dieting and people battling their weight for years, which is not a healthy way to live, and it shouldn't be accepted as the norm.

One day while I was out jogging, I decided I would do something about it. I would create an online nutrition and training plan to educate people properly and rescue them from these damaging, unhealthy diets. My aim was to create a sustainable plan with tasty meals that would get people eating more food, training more effectively (and for much less time!) and burning fat.

Everyone has different energy demands. My meal plans are unique; I create tailored meal plans that allow choice and flexibility, to ensure people get results and keep them. After months of planning, the 90 Day Shift, Shape and Sustain plan was born. I used social media to promote it, and started to post 'before' and 'after' transformation pictures, along with

'MY AIM WAS TO CREATE A SUSTAINABLE PLAN'

written testimonials. I had no idea what I had created at the time – and, to this day, I can't quite believe the success it's had. But by creating an online community, I unknowingly connected thousands of people who were all on the same journey. As more and more clients signed up online, I had to step away from my boot camps, and eventually I passed on all my personal training clients to a friend. My business was now fully online and going global.

90 DAY**SSS**   90 DAY SSS GRADUATE

Originally it was mainly people from the UK signing up, but then people all over the world started to get on board. Places as far away as Australia, Sweden, Singapore and Dubai were starting to hear about Lean in 15 and signing up to my 90 Day Shift, Shape and Sustain plan. It started off with just me answering a few emails and sending a few plans out each week, but before I knew it I had thousands of people signing up each month and a team of support staff to help coach clients on their journey.

I absolutely love what I do now, and although I never get to actually meet any of my clients, I'm really proud of all of them and feel inspired by them every day. By educating people on nutrition I have been able to empower them to take control and achieve their goals in a healthy and enjoyable way.

As The Body Coach, I am now on a mission to help even more people. It's important to note that my online business didn't just happen overnight – it grew organically and came from nothing but hard work. It takes a lot of trust for a person to buy into something without ever meeting you, and I built that trust up over hundreds of hours of interaction, videos and tweets. When no one was listening, I kept sharing and giving, and eventually people started to hear me.

So that's a little bit about me and my story up to now. I'm very excited to be sharing my knowledge and recipes with you. I hope you enjoy the book and get inspired to cook, prep like a boss and get the body you've always wanted.

Joe Wicks

– THE BODY COACH

1

THE LEAN IN 15 PLAN

DIETS DON'T WORK!

///

The problem with diets is that they don't work – not in the long term, anyway. Yes, you can lose weight initially, especially with a drastic decrease in calories, but the likelihood is that you will soon return to your old eating habits and regain any weight lost. After working with thousands of clients, I know that success only happens when a programme is enjoyable and sustainable. A meal plan needs to be easy to follow and stress-free, because life is stressful enough and we simply don't have the time to spend hours in the kitchen every day.

This is why I created Lean in 15. No matter how busy you are, you can take control and find a quarter of an hour to cook your meals and stay lean. This isn't a strict diet – it's a lifestyle that will transform your body and the way you eat forever. Once I teach you how to fuel your body properly, you will never need to follow a low-calorie diet again.

Most of the recipes in this book will be ready in less than 15 minutes, and many of them can be batch-cooked, so you can double up and prepare meals for the day or week ahead. A few of the meals take a little longer than 15 minutes so are not technically 'Lean in 15' but don't worry, it's because they taste great and will be well worth the wait! The busier you are, the

> ❛ Success only happens when a programme is enjoyable and sustainable ❜

more you will need to prep your meals. I call this 'Prepping like a boss', and it's one of the ways you can guarantee your success. I'll be sharing my top tips for prepping like a boss further on in this book, so keep a lookout.

There are no shortcuts

I want you to ignore all the adverts trying to sell you fat-burning herbal supplements, meal-replacement shakes or juice diets. They are not the solution. In fact, these diets are the problem, as they go against the basic principles of nutrition and the way metabolism works. What's more, they rely on repeat business, because they know that once you lose the weight, you'll soon regain it and be back for more of their products. I want to help you break this vicious circle once and for all.

The truth is there are no shortcuts to a lean body. It takes time, dedication, consistent training and the right nutrition. The good news is that Lean in 15 is not going to deprive you of entire food groups or leave you feeling hungry like most diets. My approach is the complete opposite. I want to encourage you to think differently and change your approach. I want you to eat *more* food, and I'm going to show you how to fuel your body properly, so you burn fat and build lean muscle. The more lean muscle you have, the more efficient your metabolism will be – and that means you can enjoy eating even more food. That's winning!

I'm also going to explain the importance of fats, proteins and carbohydrates, so you understand what to fuel your body with and when. My philosophy is simple and easy to adopt into your lifestyle.

Your body is unique

The portions in the recipes in this book are not specifically tailored to you, as it would be impossible without knowing much more about you (your current weight, activity level, age range and more). Every body has its own unique energy demands, so you will need to increase or decrease the portion sizes according to your activity levels. For example, if you train hard and have a really physically active job, you need to eat more than someone who sits at a desk for eight hours a day and does little exercise.

> ❝ I want you to eat *more* food, and I'm going to show you how to fuel your body properly ❞

It doesn't have to be difficult or complicated. You will soon start to notice if you feel energized or not, so listen to your body – and please don't go hungry! Although I can't tailor portion sizes to individual readers, the structured way of eating outlined in this book – what to eat and when – is very effective for fat loss. The structure is the same as cycle one of my 90 Day Shift, Shape and Sustain plan, which has worked brilliantly for tens of thousands of people. This phase is called the 'Shift' phase, because that's exactly what it does. It shifts unwanted fat by putting your body in fat-burning mode at all times through a combination of diet and exercise (I have also included some sample home HIIT workouts for you to try out – see page 194).

Understanding macronutrients

Our three main energy sources – fats, protein and carbohydrates – are called macronutrients. They all play an important role in helping our bodies stay lean, strong and healthy. The way of eating in this book won't cut any of these out of your diet, but rather will provide you with them in the right ratios at the right time to get the best possible response from your body.

During low-intensity activity, such as watching TV, walking to the shops and even sleeping, your body mostly uses fats to fuel itself. When working at a high intensity, it mostly uses stored carbohydrates for energy. I'm going to show you how to use this knowledge to your advantage, to ensure your body is always using the correct energy source in line with your energy demands.

Let's talk about fats

Fats have been unfairly demonized, to the extent that people now believe that all fats are bad and will make you get fat, and a whole industry has arisen around low-fat versions of common foods. Fat is often the first thing people cut out when trying to lose weight. But not all fats are the same. Some fats – such as trans-fats found in processed foods – should be avoided, but others are actually essential for the body, such as omega-3s (found in oily fish), which help reduce inflammation. These are known as essential fatty acids (EFAs), as they cannot be made in the body and so must be obtained from the diet. Fat also plays an essential role in vitamin absorption: vitamins A, D, E and K are fat-soluble, meaning your body can't absorb them without fat being present.

People also often associate energy with carbohydrates, but fats are actually the most energy-dense macronutrient of all. Fats provide your body with 9 kcal energy per gram, compared to just 4 kcal per gram from protein and carbohydrates. This makes fat an incredible energy source, and one that keeps blood sugar levels stable. Fat also takes longer to digest in the body, which means you feel satisfied for longer and are less likely to snack in between meals.

Why are fats important?

Fats have several important roles in the body, including:
★ Providing you with energy
★ Enabling the absorption of fat-soluble vitamins
★ Protecting your organs, nerves and tissues
★ Helping to regulate body temperature
★ Every cell membrane in the body needs fat for protection, and fat is also needed to grow new healthy cells
★ Fats are involved in the production of essential hormones in the body
★ Maintenance of healthy hair, skin and nails

What are the types of fat?

There are 3 types of fat:
★ Saturated – animal fats, butter, eggs, cheese, coconut oil
★ Monounsaturated – nuts, avocados, extra virgin olive oil, peanut oil, sesame oil
★ Polyunsaturated – sunflower oil, walnut oil, flaxseed oil, and oily fish such as salmon and mackerel

Saturated fats have an awful reputation, which dates back to the 1950s, when a study found that the consumption of saturated fat increased levels of bad cholesterol in the blood, and that this led to coronary heart disease. In hindsight, this research was extremely flawed and failed to take into account those countries where people had a very high intake of saturated fat and yet very low levels of heart disease. Unfortunately this 'diet-heart' hypothesis influenced government health guidelines and the low-fat food industry started to boom. Instead of fats, we were encouraged to consume more carbohydrates, such as grains, rice and pasta. But since then, deaths from obesity, diabetes and heart-related diseases have continued to rise.

Ironically, the latest research suggests that saturated fats from butter, milk, cream, eggs and coconut oil actually increase the levels of good cholesterol in the blood and benefit the heart, so there is no need to fear these foods. This doesn't mean you should sit down and eat a whole wheel of cheese, though. Fats do contain lots of calories, after all, so you need to eat everything in moderation and in line with your own personal energy demands.

Monounsaturated fats

Monounsaturated fats, found in things such as extra virgin olive oil, avocados and nuts, are great for increasing good cholesterol levels. This is one of the reasons a handful of nuts, seeds or half an avocado make a perfect snack. Unlike sugary cereal bars and chocolate, these snacks will also keep your blood sugar levels stable and sustain your energy levels for much longer.

Polyunsaturated fats

Polyunsaturated fats can be found in oily fish like salmon and mackerel and are a great source of omega-3 fatty acids. These are considered anti-inflammatory, which means they reduce your risk of injuries and chronic disease. I'm not the biggest fan of fish, and for the first 25 years of my life I wouldn't go near it, but I've slowly trained myself to eat it because I understand its importance for my health. No amount of omega-3 fish oil capsules will beat a fresh piece of wild salmon, so try to eat fish at least twice a week.

Bad fats

The hydrogenated fats we need to eliminate from our diet aren't just found in sugary sweets, pastries and fast-food restaurants. They are also hidden in many low-fat diet products. Low-fat ready meals, for example, may be low in saturated fat

> ‘ A handful of nuts, seeds or half an avocado make a perfect snack ’

but they are often loaded with hydrogenated trans-fats to increase their shelf-life. My advice is to prepare all of your own meals from scratch, avoiding ready meals wherever possible.

What should I cook with?

. . . .

You'll notice that I mostly use coconut oil or butter for cooking – this is because these saturated fats are more stable when heated to high temperatures. Processed polyunsaturated vegetable oils and margarines, on the other hand, become unstable when heated. This means they oxidize easily, producing free radicals, and these are not what you want to be putting inside your body. When free radicals attack fat molecules, they develop similar properties to a trans-fat, increasing the levels of bad cholesterol in your blood at the same time as decreasing the levels of good cholesterol – a double-whammy effect that's not great when it comes to the health of your heart.

What about protein?

. . . .

Protein forms the basis of all meals in the Lean in 15 plan, and remains consistent on both training and rest days. Protein is essential for:

★ Maintaining the structure and strength of cells and tissues
★ Regulation of metabolism
★ Production of hormones
★ Repair and growth of muscle tissues
★ Strengthening your immune system

Where should I get my protein?

. . . .

Proteins are broken down into amino acids inside the body. Many of my recipes contain animal protein sources, such as eggs, fish, chicken and beef. These are considered complete protein sources because they contain all the essential amino acids needed by the body. If you are a vegetarian you can of course use tofu or Quorn as a protein source, but you'll need to eat much larger quantities to get your protein intake to the required level.

> **Prepare all of your own meals from scratch, avoiding ready meals wherever possible**

Protein powder

I always say real food, not dust, burns fat. What I mean by this is that supplements should only be used alongside a good diet and not in place of real food. However, you may notice that in some of my recipes, such as overnight oats, I do use protein powder. Whey protein is a brilliant post-workout addition to your diet because it reaches the muscles quickly, so the amino acids can start to repair and rebuild muscle fibres immediately after a training session. If you need a dairy-free alternative (whey is derived from dairy), you could try a vegan protein powder, such as hemp or pea.

Let's talk about carbohydrates

There is so much confusion surrounding carbohydrates – which carbs are good and which are bad, and when you can and can't eat them. I'm going to clear all this up and show you what a great energy source they can be.

We've all heard the ridiculous myth that eating carbs after 6pm makes you fat. It's pure nonsense! Carbs don't make you fat. What actually makes us gain fat is when we eat over and above our bodies' energy demands. So, providing you eat the right amount each day, you will not gain fat but instead will be able to train harder and build more muscle, which will make you leaner.

Why do we need carbohydrates?

★　Carbohydrates are the main source of energy for muscles during intense exercise
★　They are needed for the proper functioning of the central nervous system, kidneys and muscles
★　Carbs also contain fibre, which is important for good intestinal health and digestion
★　They are essential for healthy brain function

The white carb police

Lots of people seem to be scared of eating white bread, pasta and rice, and attempt to ban it from their lives. I call these people 'the white carb police'. Unshakeable in their belief that you can't eat white carbs when trying to burn fat, they will eat only the brown, wholegrain versions of these carbs – but you really don't need to fear white carbs.

While it's true that wholegrain carbs have a lower glycaemic load (GL), which means they don't cause your blood sugar levels to spike as much as white carbs, after training your body actually loves high-GL foods. The higher the GL of a food, the greater will be the elevation of blood glucose levels, prompting the pancreas to release insulin. However, this insulin response is great after a workout as it means the nutrients from your carbohydrate-refuel meal are shuttled to the muscles quicker. Combining high GL carbs with low GL carbs such as table sugar with porridge oats reduces the overall GL and elevation of blood sugar levels.

In summary, if you love brown rice, eat brown rice – but if you long for a big bowl of white rice or a white bagel, then know that after you train is the ideal time to enjoy it.

How will I be eating?

. . . .

You are going to be eating in line with your energy demands. This means that you will eat differently on training days and rest days.

You are going to ensure that your body is using the correct energy source, in line with your energy demands – that is, carbohydrates after exercise, and fats as steady fuel for the remainder of your day and night, and on rest days.

The recipes in this book are broken down into 3 sections:
1. Reduced-carbohydrate meals: rich in healthy fats and protein
2. Post-workout carbohydrate-refuel meals: high in protein and carbohydrates
3. Snacks and treats: sweet and savoury snacks and tasty treats

On a training day, you will eat 2 reduced-carbohydrate meals, 1 post-workout carbohydrate-refuel meal and 2 snacks.

On a rest day, you will eat 3 reduced-carbohydrate meals and 2 snacks.

You will eat differently on training days and rest days

Why do I eat this way?

My post-workout carbohydrate-refuel meal structure is very effective for fat loss. Your body stores carbohydrates in the liver and muscles as glycogen and, after a workout, these are depleted, so you need to 'refuel' and top up those stores after training. When you consume carbohydrates, they are broken down into sugars and this increases your blood sugar levels, causing the pancreas to release insulin. Remember, this is a good thing post-workout as insulin shuttles the nutrients from your meal into your muscles quickly, so they can get to work repairing and rebuilding.

Whenever you're not working intensively, your body uses mainly fats for fuel. This is why you will reduce your carbohydrates on rest days and increase your fat intake. At first you might struggle to make this change. Psychologically you may feel like you are low on energy, but don't forget you are still providing your body with energy – just from fats instead of carbs. You will soon adjust to it, so persevere. And remember, you are eating to stay lean.

What meals should I choose?

The training plan is flexible and all meals are interchangeable. This means you could have protein pancakes for breakfast or dinner, depending on when you train. Just remember that you are 'earning' those carbs during your workout, so you must always choose a carbohydrate-refuel meal afterwards, regardless of how late you train.

If there is a recipe you want to try, but you don't like a certain ingredient, such as onions or peppers, simply swap it for something similar that you do enjoy. The same goes with the protein – for example, if you don't like beef mince, you can always use turkey mince.

I've included a few treats in the book but these should only be eaten once or twice a week and only after a workout.

Alcohol and fat loss

I'm always very honest and realistic with my clients when it comes to drinking alcohol. I never tell them to cut it out completely, as this is a personal choice for them to make. I just remind them that the less booze they drink, the leaner they will get. Put simply, alcohol puts the brakes on fat loss, as it interferes with the normal metabolic pathways, including fat-burning, in the body.

In addition to alcohol preventing you from burning fat, it also contributes a significant amount to your daily intake of calories. It's very easy to drink a lot of calories from alcohol without realizing it, and this can have a big knock-on effect on your training and nutrition the following day. With a hangover, you are not likely to want to train or to eat particularly well – personally, I'll eat everything in sight when hungover, including tubs and tubs of ice cream.

Ultimately you need to find your own balance, but if you really are serious about getting lean and transforming your body, then you will need to sacrifice a few nights out on the booze. Alcohol could well be the one thing holding you back from achieving the body you want.

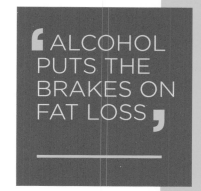

'ALCOHOL PUTS THE BRAKES ON FAT LOSS'

Hydration

Most people underestimate the importance of hydration for fat loss. Almost two thirds of the human body is made up of water, and it is involved in everything from removing waste and lubricating joints to regulating body temperature. It also aids metabolism, so consumption of water is vital to maximize your body's fat-burning ability. As a general rule, I recommend drinking between 2 and 4 litres of water per day. This may seem like a lot, but it really will work wonders for your body inside and out. If you don't enjoy drinking plain water, try adding some fresh mint, lemon or lime for a bit of flavour.

GETTING STARTED

2

Olive Oil

Soy Sauce

Oats

Cinnamon

Curry powder

Garam Masala

Chilli flakes

FAIT MAISON

Chopped Tomatoes

Pine nuts

Coconut oil

Coconut Milk

GETTING STARTED

///

> **No more low calories, zero carbs or low fat for you**

Hopefully you now have a better understanding of macro-nutrients and how you are going to use them to fuel your body to get lean. No more low calories, zero carbs or low fat for you! You are going to eat lots of tasty food, feel full of energy every day, and really give your body a chance to transform.

STEP 1:
PLAN LIKE A WINNER

Planning your meals and workouts into the week ahead is the first step for success. You may not be able to follow it 100%, as things will inevitably pop up during the week that are beyond your control. That's life, but it's still important to set yourself daily goals: if you can only manage 3 workouts per week, then that's what you should put in your plan. Keep it realistic and achievable, as small daily wins will increase your motivation to follow your plan.

Start by writing down your workouts and meals into a table like mine on page 214. This will allow you to schedule time for your workouts and also create a shopping list ready for when you prep your meals.

PREPPING LIKE A BOSS

Now you have planned like a winner it's time to get your food shopping done and get prepping like a boss. This means spending a couple of hours in the kitchen on a weekend to set yourself up for success. It may seem like a hassle to begin with, but you will get quicker and more organized, and soon it will become an easy habit for you. It's a great feeling to know exactly what you are fuelling your body with, and it means you can avoid buying junk food on the go when you get hungry. You can leave the house with your lunch sorted and your dinner all ready to go, so that after a long day at work or a late session at the gym, you can just stroll in, reheat your meal and refuel your body quickly.

The busier your lifestyle and job is, the further in advance you will need to prep. Some people like to cook and freeze their meals for a week ahead. I personally prefer to eat a bit fresher, so I just prep my meals a day or two in advance and keep them in the fridge. I then either eat them cold or reheat them in the microwave or oven. There is no right or wrong way to do this. Just keep it as stress-free as possible and make it fit your lifestyle – that way you're more likely to stick to it and form good habits.

> ❝ I just prep my meals a day or two in advance and keep them in the fridge ❞

STEP 3:

GET STOCKED UP!

Now you know how to prep like a boss, you need a few essential tools and ingredients to start putting your plans into action:

1. Food scales – to weigh your ingredients and maintain good portion control

2. Food storage containers – to store and organize all your tasty meals for the week ahead

3. A decent wok and pan – there's nothing worse than a bad wok, so invest in a good one

4. Store cupboard essentials – some core ingredients in the cupboard or fridge, so you don't get caught out

5. A refillable water bottle – to ensure you stay hydrated at all times and can keep track of your water intake each day.

STORE CUPBOARD ESSENTIALS

////////////////////////////////

Garam masala
Curry powder
Fresh root ginger
Ground cinnamon
Garlic
Chilli flakes
Pine nuts
Tinned tomatoes
Oats
Light soy sauce
Olive oil
Coconut oil
Coconut milk

THROW AWAY THE SAD STEP!

////////////////////////////////

I call bathroom scales the sad step because that's exactly what they are: you stand on them every day, and then feel sad when the numbers aren't moving in the right direction. This often results in people losing motivation, bingeing on junk food or quitting a plan altogether. I don't want you to be concerned with the numbers any more.

The truth is, when it comes to hitting your health and fitness goals, the sad step is the worst measure of success you can possibly get and it's time you threw it out the window. Because no matter how hard you train, or how well you eat, scales cannot measure some of the most important things when it comes to your body, health and wellbeing.

> ' I don't want you to be concerned with the numbers any more '

Things the sad step CANNOT measure:

Your fitness levels
Your energy levels
Your strength
Changes in your body composition
Your sense of achievement
Your confidence
Your happiness

The best motivational tool for measuring your progress is taking photos of your body. My advice is to take some photos at the end of each month: these will show your true progress and keep you motivated to carry on, even when the mirror starts playing tricks on you and you convince yourself you haven't changed.

GO GET LEAN

Once you've got your meals and workouts planned, you can start your journey to a fitter, stronger and leaner version of yourself. Remember, fat loss is a journey not a race, so be patient and be consistent.

LET'S GET SOCIAL

If you want to see more recipes or share your meals and progress with me, post and tag your pics with the hashtag #Leanin15 on Twitter, Instagram and Facebook @thebodycoach.

For more HIIT workouts, check out my YouTube channel TheBodyCoachTV.

> ' Fat loss is a journey not a race ,

REDUCED-CARBOHYDRATE RECIPES

3

NUT AND MANGO SMOOTHIE

This fruity smoothie is ideal for a last-minute breakfast on the go. With healthy fats and a scoop of protein powder, this is way better for you than any bowl of boxed cereal. Try not to get into the habit of having smoothies every day, though. As I always say, real food wins over dust every time.

INGREDIENTS

125g sliced mango
2 tbsp almond or cashew
  butter
handful of ice cubes
handful of raspberries
2 tbsp full-fat Greek yoghurt
1 scoop (30g) vanilla or
  strawberry protein powder
100ml almond milk

METHOD

Place all the ingredients in a blender and blend until smooth.

★ TOP TIP

Warning! Don't go nuts with your nuts. While they are a great source of protein, fibre and essential fats, nuts also contain lots of calories. It's very easy to crack open a 200g bag and finish the lot without feeling full. But remember every gram of fat contains 9 kcal, so overeating nuts will not help with your fat loss. I recommend a snack portion of 25–30g. Also, try to get a variety of different nuts as they contain different vitamins. Almonds, walnuts and cashews are my personal favourites.

FATS-ME-UP SMOOTHIE

SERVES 1

Here's another tasty low-carb smoothie you can drink on the go. The almond milk and avocado provide you with some healthy fats for fuel, but feel free to add a scoop of your favourite protein too for an extra boost. Make sure you use a soft, ripe avocado for this.

INGREDIENTS

juice of 2 limes
200ml almond milk
handful of blackberries
handful of blueberries
½ avocado, roughly chopped
3 tbsp full-fat Greek yoghurt
1 tbsp honey

METHOD

Throw everything into a blender and blitz until smooth.

★ TOP TIP

The avocado is a nutritional hero in my eyes, with a long list of health benefits. It's a great source of monounsaturated oleic acid, which research has shown reduces levels of bad LDL cholesterol at the same time as increasing levels of the more beneficial HDL cholesterol. That means this little rascal is actually good for your heart.

SERVES 1

CINNAMON REDUCED-CARB OATMEAL

I always like to encourage people to think outside the cereal box at breakfast but there's nothing wrong with a good bowl of oats. The added chia and flaxseeds in this meal provide a dose of those all-important and essential omega-3 fatty acids. This one will leave you feeling full and energized until lunch.

INGREDIENTS

22g chia seeds

22g golden flaxseed meal

40g finely shredded unsweetened coconut

30g oats – rolled or steel-cut, not instant

¾ tsp ground cinnamon

300ml almond milk, plus a little extra if needed

3 tbsp full-fat Greek yoghurt

METHOD

Place all the ingredients except the yoghurt in a small saucepan and cook gently over low heat for 5–6 minutes until you're happy with the consistency – add a little more almond milk if the oatmeal gets too thick.

Transfer to a bowl, dollop the yoghurt on top and serve.

★ TOP TIP

Flaxseeds (also called linseeds) are a rich source of micronutrients, dietary fibre, vitamin B1 and an omega-3 fatty acid called alpha-linoleic acid (ALA). So if you don't enjoy eating oily fish, try to get flaxseeds into your diet more often.

SERVES 1

GO-GO-GREEN SMOOTHIE

Mums always tell us to eat our greens, so here you go. If you're not a big fan of leafy green veg, then this is the perfect opportunity for you to smash them in. Wheatgrass is very good for you – but, just like Marmite, it's a love or hate kind of thing. If you don't enjoy it, just leave it out and add more spinach or some kale instead.

INGREDIENTS

175ml coconut water

2 tbsp almond butter

25g fresh wheatgrass (or 5g powdered)

1 scoop (30g) vanilla protein powder

1 apple, cored and roughly chopped

20g flaxseeds

handful of baby spinach leaves

handful of ice cubes

METHOD

Put all the ingredients in a blender and blend on high for 1 minute or until the smoothie has reached your desired texture.

CAULIFLOWER COUSCOUS CHICKEN SALAD

SERVES 2

In my opinion, cauliflower is underrated and underused. It's extremely nutritious and full of goodness. Use this recipe as a basis to experiment with other flavour combinations – try it with smoked mackerel instead of chicken, for example. If you want a warm dish, just microwave the cauliflower on its own and then add the other ingredients.

MAKE AHEAD
INGREDIENTS

1 cauliflower, broken into florets

4 tbsp pomegranate seeds

5 sundried tomatoes, roughly chopped

2 jarred red peppers, roughly chopped

2 tbsp walnut oil or olive oil

4 tbsp walnuts, roughly chopped

½ bunch of chives, finely sliced

½ bunch of parsley, leaves only, roughly chopped

large handful of baby spinach leaves

400g cooked skinless chicken breast (deli chicken is perfect)

juice of 1 lemon

METHOD

Place the cauliflower florets in a food processor and pulse until they have a couscous-like texture.

Tip your cauliflower couscous into a large bowl and add all the other ingredients except the chicken and lemon juice. Mix the whole lot thoroughly.

Pile up your couscous on plates, then top with the cooked chicken and a good squeeze of lemon juice.

CHEESY CHORIZO CHICKEN AND SPINACH

This is pretty much the simplest dish you can imagine. And melted cheese is sooooo satisfying! You can also try this with prawns or turkey mince for a change, if you like.

INGREDIENTS

½ tbsp coconut oil
75g chorizo, finely diced
½ red onion, diced
1 x 240g skinless chicken
  breast fillet, cut into
  1cm slices
salt and pepper
4 cherry tomatoes, sliced
  in half
3 big fistfuls of baby
  spinach leaves
1 ball of mozzarella, torn
  into chunks
20g pine nuts

METHOD

Heat the coconut oil in a large frying pan over a medium to high heat. Add the chorizo and fry for a minute. Add the onion and fry for another minute.

Increase the heat to maximum and add the chicken, along with a generous pinch of both salt and pepper. Stir-fry for about 3 minutes, by which time the chicken should be almost completely cooked through.

Throw in the cherry tomatoes and cook for a minute or until they just begin to collapse. Toss in the spinach and stir through until fully wilted.

Use a wooden spoon to make little pockets in the chicken and vegetable mixture, then drop in small chunks of the mozzarella. Turn off the heat and let the mozzarella melt before spooning the whole delicious lot onto a plate and scattering over the pine nuts.

CHICKEN WITH CREAMY WILD MUSHROOM AND TARRAGON SAUCE

GOOD TO FREEZE
INGREDIENTS

2 x 225g skinless chicken
  breast fillets
1 tbsp olive oil
1 clove garlic, finely chopped
300g mixed mushrooms –
  I like chestnut and oyster
splash of white wine
2 large handfuls of baby
  spinach leaves
150ml double cream
½ bunch of tarragon, leaves
  only, roughly chopped
salt and pepper

This old-school classic really hits the spot: it's so full of flavour, and poaching the chicken keeps it nice and moist. Most supermarkets now stock some great wild mushrooms, so be adventurous and get some exotic-looking ones.

METHOD

Bring a large saucepan of water to the boil, then slide in the chicken. Lower the heat until the water is just 'burping' and not vigorously boiling. Let the chicken cook for 12 minutes, by which time it should be fully cooked through.

Meanwhile, heat the oil in a large frying pan over a medium to high heat. Add the garlic and cook for about 30 seconds. Roughly chop any larger mushrooms and throw them into the pan, to give them a head start for a minute or two before adding the rest of the mushrooms and cooking for another minute.

Increase the heat to maximum, then pour in the white wine and let it bubble away to almost nothing. Drop in the spinach and stir until wilted. Pour in the double cream, then bring to the boil and simmer for 1 minute. Add the chopped tarragon and remove the pan from the heat.

Check that the chicken is cooked by slicing into the thickest part of the breast: the meat should be white all the way through and the juices should run clear, not pink. Remove to a plate, draining off as much liquid as possible. Season with salt and pepper, then place on two plates and pour over the delicious creamy sauce.

★ Serve with a big portion of your favourite greens such as spinach, kale, broccoli, mange tout or green beans.

MAKE AHEAD
GOOD TO FREEZE
(if freezing, increase the
amount of stock to 150ml)

INGREDIENTS

2 tsp coconut oil
2 shallots, finely sliced
5 chestnut mushrooms,
  roughly chopped
300g fillet steak, cut into 1cm
  thick strips
salt and pepper
2 tsp smoked paprika
75ml beef stock
125ml soured cream
½ bunch of parsley, leaves
  only, roughly chopped –
  optional
juice of 1 lemon

SUPER-SPEEDY BEEF STROGANOFF

Fillet steak is the best cut for this dish, but it is expensive,
so if you're on a budget opt for sirloin or rump. If you love
steak then this one is a real winner.

METHOD

Melt the coconut oil in a frying pan over a high heat.
Add the shallots and mushrooms and fry, stirring regularly,
for 2–3 minutes or until the shallots have softened and the
mushrooms have taken on a little colour.

Add the beef, along with a generous pinch of both salt and
pepper, and stir-fry for 1–2 minutes. Sprinkle in the smoked
paprika and toss to lightly coat everything with the spice.

Pour in the beef stock – it will bubble up quickly – then turn
the heat right down and stir in the soured cream. Take the
pan off the heat, then add the parsley, if using, and a generous
squeeze of lemon juice. Serve and enjoy.

★ Serve with a big portion of your favourite greens such as
spinach, kale, broccoli, mange tout or green beans.

MAKE AHEAD

INGREDIENTS

1 egg
75g green beans, trimmed
½ tbsp coconut oil
1 x 300g tuna fillet
salt and pepper
2 tbsp pre-cooked puy lentils
large handful of baby
  spinach leaves
1 tbsp sundried tomatoes
  (about 6)
20g walnuts, roughly chopped
1 tbsp olive oil
2 tsp balsamic or sherry
  vinegar

FRESH TUNA NIÇOISE

I love using fresh tuna for this salad, as it tastes amazing, but if you'd rather use tinned tuna, that's fine too. This makes a great packed lunch to carry to work.

METHOD

Bring a medium-sized saucepan of water to the boil before carefully lowering in the egg. Boil for 8 minutes, then drop in the green beans and simmer for a further minute.

Meanwhile, heat the coconut oil in a frying pan over a medium to high heat. Carefully lay in the tuna and fry for 1 minute on each side. This will give you rare tuna – if you like it more cooked, fry it for a further minute on each side. Remove the tuna from the pan, season and leave to rest while you put the rest of the salad together.

Drain the egg and beans in a sieve or colander, then run under cold water until cool enough to handle. Peel the egg and slice in half. Put the beans, lentils, spinach, sundried tomatoes, walnuts, olive oil and vinegar into a bowl, along with a generous pinch of salt and pepper. Gently toss all the ingredients together, then transfer to a plate.

Top the salad with the tuna, sliced if you like, and the egg.

ASIAN DUCK SALAD

Duck is a rich and delicious meat that's packed with protein. For the veg, I've gone with asparagus and midget trees (my name for broccoli!), but feel free to improvise. Having fun in the kitchen and mixing it up will help to keep things tasty and vary your nutrients. As you can see, I've doubled the recipe in the picture.

SERVES 1

MAKE AHEAD
INGREDIENTS

5 spears of asparagus
4 midget trees (tender-stem broccoli), any bigger stalks sliced in half lengthways
½ tbsp coconut oil
1 x 250g duck breast fillet, sliced into 1cm thick strips
2cm ginger, finely chopped
1 tbsp light soy sauce
2 tsp sesame oil
2 tbsp ready-cooked quinoa
1 spring onion, finely sliced
¼ cucumber, sliced into thin batons

METHOD

Take each asparagus spear in turn and bend it gently until it snaps – it will naturally snap at the point where it becomes tender. Discard the bottom of the spear.

Bring a large saucepan of water to the boil, then drop in the asparagus and the midget trees and simmer for 1½ minutes. Drain in a sieve or colander, then rinse under cold running water.

Melt the coconut oil in a frying pan over a high heat. Add the duck and stir-fry for 30 seconds, then add the ginger and stir-fry for a further minute, by which time the duck should be cooked through. Remove the pan from the heat and stir through the soy sauce and sesame oil.

Place the cooked vegetables in a bowl, then add the quinoa and the duck, along with all its juices. Mix the whole lot together before transferring to a plate and topping with the spring onion and cucumber.

THAI GREEN CURRY

This tasty classic is my all-time favourite meal. In this version I've suggested prawns, but chicken and pork would work just as well. Bump up the flavour by using full-fat coconut milk, which is packed with good fat. Fish sauce is great to have in the cupboard: it keeps for ages, and even though it smells terrible, it tastes amazing.

MAKE AHEAD
GOOD TO FREEZE
INGREDIENTS

2 tbsp coconut oil

2 star anise

1 small aubergine, chopped into small pieces

2 tbsp Thai green curry paste

1 x 400ml tin of full-fat coconut milk

handful of baby sweetcorn

450g raw king prawns, peeled

1–2 tbsp fish sauce

3 limes

½ bunch of basil, leaves only, roughly chopped

½ bunch of coriander, leaves only, roughly chopped

1 red chilli, roughly chopped – remove the seeds if you don't like it hot

METHOD

Melt the coconut oil in a large saucepan over a medium to high heat. Add the star anise and aubergine and fry for 1 minute, then add in the curry paste (store-bought is fine) and half the coconut milk. Stir the paste into the milk, then increase the heat to maximum.

Pour in the rest of the coconut milk, then half-fill the tin with water, slosh it around and pour this into the pan as well. Toss in the sweetcorn, then bring to the boil and simmer for 3 minutes. Drop in the prawns and simmer for a further 2 minutes until they turn pink and are fully cooked.

Take the pan off the heat and chuck in the fish sauce to taste, the juice of 2 of the limes, the herbs and the chilli.

Serve up the curry in bowls, with the last lime cut into quarters for squeezing.

★ TOP TIP

Here's my recipe to make your own Thai green curry paste:

4 banana shallots, peeled and chopped

4cm galangal, peeled and chopped

4 cloves garlic, peeled and chopped

2 stalks lemongrass, trimmed and chopped

1 tsp cumin seeds

½ tsp coriander seeds

1 bunch of basil

2 bunches of coriander

1 tbsp fish sauce

pinch of grated star anise

Blend the whole lot together using either a little warm water or coconut milk to loosen. You can keep this in an airtight container in the fridge for up to 5 days.

SERVES 1

MAKE AHEAD
GOOD TO FREEZE

INGREDIENTS

20g butter
2 rashers of smoked streaky
  bacon, cut into 1cm strips
½ red onion, diced
1 clove garlic, finely chopped
250g cod fillet, skinned and
  cut into 2cm chunks
1 x 400g tin chopped
  tomatoes
8 pitted black olives
1 ball of mozzarella, torn
  into chunks
20g pine nuts
basil leaves, to serve –
  optional

FRENCH STYLE COD WITH BLACK OLIVES

This is a simple and delicious dish based on a classic French combo. If you're not a fan of cod, you could use any other white fish of your choice.

METHOD

Melt the butter in a large frying pan over a medium to high heat. Add the bacon and onion and fry for 2 minutes or until the onion is starting to soften and the bacon is cooked. Add the garlic and cook for a further 30 seconds.

Drop in the chunks of cod and fry, turning the chunks every now and then, for 2 minutes. Add the tomatoes and bring to the boil. Reduce the heat to a simmer and cook for 2–3 minutes.

Add the olives and mozzarella, then take the pan off the heat and let the mozzarella melt in the residual heat.

Serve the cod topped with the pine nuts – and the basil leaves, if using.

EGGS BAKED IN AVOCADO

**SERVES
1**

INGREDIENTS

4 rashers of smoked back
  bacon
1 ripe avocado
2 eggs
salt and pepper
1 red chilli, finely sliced –
  remove the seeds if you
  don't like it hot

This is becoming a bit of a signature dish for me. I've posted it a few times, and I love seeing people make it at home and share it on Instagram. It contains more healthy fats than you can shake a stick at . . . oh, and it's got bacon too, so you know it's going to taste as good as it looks.

METHOD

Preheat your grill to maximum, then lay the bacon on the grill pan or a baking tray and slide underneath. Grill for 3 minutes on each side for crispy bacon.

Meanwhile, cut your avocado in half, remove the stone and scoop out a generous tablespoon of flesh from each half to create a hole big enough for the egg. No need to waste the leftover avocado – you can save it to make some guacamole or just eat it on the spot!

Crack an egg into each avocado half, pierce each egg white in a couple of places, season with a little salt and pepper and place on a microwaveable plate. Cook the eggs in 30-second bursts for 2 minutes – this should ensure firm whites, but runny yolks. Leave to stand for 1 minute.

Serve up the baked eggs and avocado with the bacon and a scattering of chilli.

★ TOP TIP

To stop the avocados rocking on the plate, slice off a little bit underneath to make a flat base.

INDIAN SPICED LAMB

This is proper dinner-party food! You can see I've doubled the recipe in the picture. Make sure you buy cutlets not chops, because they have a better meat-to-fat ratio. And if you have any leftovers (not likely!), they are delicious the next day, served at room temperature with a big salad.

MAKE AHEAD

INGREDIENTS

150g natural yoghurt
2 tbsp ground almonds
2 tsp garam masala
1 tsp smoked paprika
salt and pepper
4 lamb cutlets, about
　　200g each
large handful of baby
　　spinach leaves
4 cherry tomatoes, halved
¼ cucumber, sliced into
　　batons
½ bunch of coriander, leaves
only, roughly chopped
juice of 1 lemon

METHOD

Preheat your grill to maximum and line a baking tray with baking parchment (this is just to make washing up easier).

Place the yoghurt, ground almonds, garam masala and smoked paprika in a bowl, along with a generous amount of salt and pepper. Mix thoroughly.

Smother the lamb cutlets with the spiced yoghurt, then place on the prepared baking tray. Slide the tray under the grill and cook the cutlets for 3–4 minutes on each side, by which time the spiced yoghurt should have browned in a few places.

Meanwhile, make a quick salad by gently tossing the spinach, tomatoes and cucumber together in a bowl. Pile the salad onto a plate.

Remove the lamb cutlets from the grill and leave to rest for 1 or 2 minutes, then sit them on top of the salad. Serve up with a scattering of coriander and a squeeze of lemon juice.

★ Serve with a big portion of your favourite greens such as kale, broccoli, mange tout or green beans.

SERVES 1

CHICKEN WITH SMOKED PAPRIKA AND ALMONDS

This is Spanish cooking at its best. I love the combo of almonds and paprika! It's really tasty and so easy to make.

MAKE AHEAD

INGREDIENTS

½ tbsp coconut oil
½ red onion, finely chopped
1 clove garlic, finely chopped
1 red pepper, de-seeded and sliced
2 tsp smoked paprika
1 tsp dried oregano
1 x 240g skinless chicken breast fillet, sliced into 1cm thick strips
5 cherry tomatoes, cut in half
20g blanched almonds
large handful of baby spinach leaves
salt and pepper
juice of 1 lemon

METHOD

Melt the coconut oil in a large frying pan over a medium to high heat. Add the onion, garlic and red pepper and fry, stirring regularly, for 2 minutes or until the vegetables are just starting to soften.

Sprinkle in the smoked paprika and oregano and stir to coat the vegetables, then increase the heat to high. Add the chicken and tomatoes and cook, still stirring regularly, for 3–4 minutes or until the chicken is fully cooked through. Check by slicing into one of the larger pieces to make sure the meat is white all the way through, with no raw pink bits left.

Stir in the almonds and spinach, then cook for a further 2 minutes, or until the spinach has totally wilted.

Plate up your chicken, season generously with salt and pepper, and finish with a squeeze of lemon juice.

★ Serve with a big portion of your favourite greens such as spinach, kale, broccoli, mange tout or green beans.

SALMON WITH CHILLI EDAMAME

SERVES 1

Edamame (soy beans) are now available already podded and frozen, so take advantage of them! This salad is high in omega-3 fatty acids to keep you lean and healthy – and it makes a perfect packed lunch.

MAKE AHEAD
INGREDIENTS

1 x 250g salmon fillet,
  skin on
200g frozen edamame
  (soy beans)
1 red chilli, finely diced –
  remove the seeds if you
  don't like it hot
1 tsp honey
2 tsp fish sauce
1 tbsp light soy sauce
2 tsp sesame oil
2 spring onions, finely sliced
1 red pepper, de-seeded and
  sliced
25g walnuts
handful of rocket leaves

METHOD

Bring two saucepans of water to the boil, then slide the salmon fillet into one and drop the edamame into the other. Simmer the edamame for 1½ minutes, then drain in a sieve or colander and rinse under cold running water. Poach the salmon for 12 minutes, or until just cooked through. Using a slotted spoon, carefully lift out the fish and place on a plate. When it is cool enough to handle, peel off the skin.

Meanwhile, mix together the chilli, honey, fish sauce, soy sauce, sesame oil and spring onions to make a dressing.

Tip the edamame into a bowl and add the red pepper, walnuts and rocket. Pour over the dressing and toss the whole lot together.

Place the salad on a plate and serve the salmon on top. This tastes great still warm from the cooking or at room temperature – you decide!

MAKE AHEAD

INGREDIENTS

½ tbsp coconut oil
1 x 250g sirloin steak,
  trimmed of visible fat
salt and pepper
1 tbsp fish sauce
juice of 2 limes
1 lemongrass stalk, tender
  white part only, finely sliced
1 red chilli, finely sliced –
  remove the seeds if you
  don't like it hot
2 tsp sesame oil
¼ cucumber, sliced into
  thin batons
2 spring onions, finely sliced
1 avocado, finely sliced
4 cherry tomatoes, cut in half
1 baby gem lettuce, leaves
  separated
20g peanuts, roughly chopped
mint and coriander leaves,
  to serve

THAI BEEF SALAD

This is also fantastic with prawns or chicken instead of
the beef. You can make up a big batch of the dressing
and keep it in the fridge for up to 3 days.

METHOD

Heat the coconut oil in a frying pan over a high heat.
Season the steak all over with salt and pepper. When the oil
has melted and is hot, carefully lay the steak in the pan and
fry for 2 minutes on each side. When the steak has had its
time, transfer it to a plate and leave to rest for 2 minutes.

While the steak is cooking, make a dressing by mixing
together the fish sauce, lime juice, lemongrass, chilli and
sesame oil in a large bowl. Stir in the cucumber and spring
onions, then leave to sit for 2 minutes.

When you are ready to eat, add the avocado, tomatoes and
lettuce to the bowl with the dressing, cucumber and spring
onions, and gently toss the whole lot together.

Pile up your salad on a plate, slice your steak and place
lovingly on the salad, before finishing with the chopped
peanuts and roughly torn coriander and mint.

TUNA STEAK WITH SALSA

SERVES 1

If you're not a fan of tinned tuna, then get your hands on a fresh tuna steak. This sort of meal is as good for you as it tastes: the tuna is stacked with protein, and the avocado fuels your body with the healthy fats it needs.

INGREDIENTS

1 x 300g tuna steak
salt and pepper
1 tbsp coconut oil
2 spring onions, finely sliced
2 tbsp tinned black-eyed
   beans
1 avocado, roughly diced
½ mango (about 100g),
   roughly diced
1 small tomato, roughly diced
1 tbsp olive oil
juice of 1 lime
¼ bunch of coriander, leaves
   only, roughly chopped

METHOD

Season the tuna generously with salt and pepper. Melt the oil in a frying pan or griddle pan over a high heat. Gently lay the tuna in the pan and cook for about 2 minutes on each side, or until it's done to your liking. Be careful not to overcook it, as tuna is lean and dries out easily. Transfer the tuna to a plate and leave to rest while you prepare the salsa.

To make the salsa, simply mix together all the remaining ingredients and taste for seasoning.

Spoon the salsa over your perfect tuna steak.

QUICK POACHED SALMON WITH SPEEDY RAT-A-TAT-A-TOUILLE

SERVES 2

MAKE AHEAD
GOOD TO FREEZE
(only the ratatouille, not the fish)

INGREDIENTS

1 tbsp coconut oil
1 small red onion, roughly diced
1 small courgette, cut into 1cm pieces
1 small aubergine, cut into 1cm pieces
1 sprig of thyme
1 tbsp tomato puree
2 tsp balsamic vinegar
2 x 250g skinless salmon fillets

Ratatouille doesn't have to take ages! Just make sure you chop all the vegetables to roughly the same, small size, so they cook quickly and evenly.

METHOD

Bring a large saucepan of water to the boil, ready to poach the salmon.

Meanwhile, melt the coconut oil in a large saucepan over a medium to high heat. Add the onion, courgette and aubergine and stir-fry for about 4 minutes or until they are just starting to soften and colour.

Drop in the thyme and stir for another minute, then squeeze in the tomato puree and mix to coat the vegetables. Keep frying, stirring continuously, for about 45 seconds before pouring in the balsamic vinegar and 100ml of water. Bring to the boil, then reduce to a simmer and let the ratatouille bubble away for about 10 minutes, or just until the vegetables are soft. If it seems to be getting too thick, add another 50ml or so of water.

While the veggies are simmering away, slide the salmon fillets into the boiling water. Bring back to a simmer, then cook the fish for 10 minutes, or until just cooked through.

Using a slotted spoon, carefully lift the fish out of the water and drain well. Serve up your yummy ratatouille topped with the juicy salmon.

TURKEY MINCE LETTUCE BOATS

SERVES 2 (makes about 12 boats)

Spicy, fiery and packed with flavour, these little boats work as well for a dinner party as they do for a quick lunch. If you're bored of turkey mince, try making these with beef mince or prawns instead.

MAKE AHEAD

INGREDIENTS

1 tbsp coconut oil
500g turkey mince
5 spring onions, finely sliced
2 cloves garlic, finely chopped
1 red chilli, finely sliced – remove the seeds if you don't like it hot
1 tbsp fish sauce
juice of 1 lime
small bunch of coriander, leaves only, roughly chopped
2 avocados, roughly chopped
2 tomatoes, roughly chopped
2–3 baby gem lettuces, leaves separated

METHOD

Heat the coconut oil in a large frying pan over a high heat. Add the turkey mince and fry for 2–3 minutes, breaking up the mince as you cook. Add the spring onions, garlic and chilli and stir-fry for another 2 minutes, by which time the turkey mince should be cooked through. Add the fish sauce, lime juice and coriander. Mix everything together well, then remove the pan from the heat.

Combine the avocados and tomatoes in a bowl.

Lay out the lettuce leaves like little boats on your serving plate, then spoon in the turkey mixture and top with the avocados and tomatoes. Now go to munchies town and enjoy.

SERVES 2

MAKE AHEAD
GOOD TO FREEZE

INGREDIENTS

12 chipolata sausages
1 tbsp olive oil
1 tsp fennel seeds
2 shallots, roughly diced
1 clove garlic, roughly
  chopped
1 sprig of thyme
2 fennel bulbs, roughly diced
2 celery sticks, roughly diced
1 courgette, roughly diced
6 cherry tomatoes
1 tbsp tomato puree
250ml chicken stock
½ bunch of parsley, leaves
  only, roughly chopped

ITALIAN STALLION SAUSAGES

Oooh, if you love a bit of sausage, then this one's for you. It requires a few more ingredients than most of my Lean in 15 meals, but it's well worth the extra effort. This makes enough for two – or a meal for one, with the leftovers boxed up for the next day.

METHOD

Preheat your grill to maximum. Line up your chipolatas on the grill pan and cook for about 5 minutes on each side or until well browned and cooked through. Check by slicing into one of the sausages to make sure there are no raw pink bits left.

While the chipolatas are cooking, heat the oil in a large saucepan and fry the fennel seeds for about 20 seconds until they smell toasty. Add the shallots, garlic, thyme, fennel, celery and courgette and stir-fry for 2 minutes or until just starting to soften. Add the tomatoes and the tomato puree and keep stirring for another minute.

Pour in the chicken stock and bring to the boil, then reduce to a simmer. Slip the cooked chipolatas into the pan and let the whole lot bubble away for a minute. Stir through the parsley, then dish up.

★ Serve with a big portion of your favourite greens such as spinach, kale, broccoli, mange tout or green beans.

CREAMY STEAK AND SPINACH

OMG – steak, wine and double cream? Am I dreaming? It feels naughty, but you'll love the taste of this one, and it's packed with healthy fats and protein.

INGREDIENTS

2 tbsp olive oil
2 x 250–300g sirloin steaks, trimmed of visible fat
salt and pepper
8 mushrooms, roughly chopped
splash of white wine
4 large handfuls of baby spinach leaves
75ml double cream

METHOD

Heat a frying pan over a high heat. Drizzle 1 tablespoon of the olive oil over the steaks, rubbing it into the flesh, and season all over with salt and pepper. Lay the steaks in the hot frying pan and cook for 3 minutes on each side. This will give you medium rare steak – if you prefer your meat medium or well done, increase the time until it's cooked to your liking. When you are happy with your steak, remove it from the frying pan and leave it to rest on a plate while you make your creamy side dish.

Wipe out the frying pan with a little kitchen roll, pour in the remaining olive oil and place over a medium to high heat. Add the mushrooms and cook, flipping them a couple of times, for 1–2 minutes or until lightly coloured. Season with salt and pepper and crank the heat up to maximum.

Pour in the white wine, and let it bubble away to almost nothing. Add the spinach and gently turn it in the pan until it is almost fully wilted. Pour in the double cream and let it bubble up. Check the seasoning and add more salt and pepper if needed.

Take a minute to look at what a delicious meal you've made, before wolfing it down!

MAKE AHEAD
INGREDIENTS

½ tbsp coconut oil

1 small red onion, diced

1 green chilli, finely chopped – remove the seeds if you don't like it hot

1 red or yellow pepper, de-seeded and sliced

½ courgette, diced

300g reduced-fat (about 5%) beef mince

1 tsp smoked paprika

2 tsp ground cumin

salt and pepper

1 tbsp full-fat Greek yoghurt

½ avocado, sliced

½ bunch of coriander, leaves only, roughly chopped – optional

CHILLI CON AVOCADO

This is a 'chuck everything in the pan' kinda dish: super-simple and tasty! It tastes great cold too, perfect for a packed lunch.

METHOD

Heat the coconut oil in a large frying pan over a high heat. Add the onion, chilli, pepper and courgette and stir-fry for 1–2 minutes or until the vegetables start to soften and colour.

Add the beef mince and stir to combine with the other ingredients, using your spoon to break up any large lumps as you go. Keep frying for about 3 minutes, by which time the mince should be fully cooked through.

Add the paprika and cumin, along with a generous pinch of salt and pepper, and cook for 30 seconds more.

Tip out your chilli onto a plate, then top with the yoghurt, avocado and coriander, if using, and serve.

SERVES 2

MAKE AHEAD
GOOD TO FREEZE

INGREDIENTS

3 cloves garlic, roughly
  chopped
3cm ginger, roughly chopped
1 green chilli, roughly
  chopped – remove the seeds
  if you don't like it hot
2 tomatoes, roughly chopped
1 tbsp coconut oil
1 red onion, diced
1 tbsp garam masala
1 tbsp ground cumin
1 x 400ml tin of full-fat
  coconut milk
500g haddock fillet, skinned
  and cut into large chunks
juice of 1 lime
½ bunch of coriander, leaves
  only, roughly chopped

GOAN FISH CURRY

You don't need to go to India to enjoy a good curry.
This recipe is surprisingly easy, but tastes incredible.
If you're not fond of fish, you could always use 250g of
skinless chicken breast fillet instead. This is a good meal to
batch-cook and freeze when you're prepping like a boss . . .

METHOD

Blitz the garlic, ginger, chilli and tomatoes in a food
processor until smooth, then leave to one side.

Melt the oil in a wok or large frying pan over a medium to
high heat. Throw in the onion and fry for 2 minutes, stirring
regularly. Sprinkle in the garam masala and cumin and fry,
stirring continuously, for 30 seconds. Pour in the blitzed
ingredients and bring to the boil before pouring in the
coconut milk. Return to the boil again, then let it simmer
for 2 minutes.

Add the haddock pieces to the curry, and bring back to a
simmer. Cook the fish for about 3 minutes, or until it is just
cooked through.

Stir in the lime juice and coriander, then serve.

TOMATOES, EGGS AND CHORIZO

SERVES 1

If you love chorizo, this is perfect for you. Frying the chorizo with the tomatoes brings out all of the delicious flavour, and the eggs provide a dose of healthy fats.

INGREDIENTS

½ tbsp olive oil
75g chorizo (the cured type, not the softer cooking chorizo), chopped
pinch of chilli flakes
2 spring onions, finely sliced
1 x 400g tin of chopped tomatoes
2 eggs
2 tbsp finely grated parmesan
sprinkling of chopped parsley, if you're feeling fancy

METHOD

Heat the oil in a small frying pan. Add the chorizo, chilli flakes and spring onions and fry for about 2 minutes, stirring regularly.

Pour in the tomatoes and bring to the boil, then simmer for 1 minute. Reduce the heat to medium to low and use the back of a spoon to fashion two dips in the tomatoes as best you can. Crack an egg into each dip, sprinkle the parmesan over the eggs and place a lid on top (if you don't have a lid for your pan, a big dinner plate or a sheet of foil should work). Simmer for about 5–6 minutes or until the whites are cooked, but the yolks are still runny.

Sprinkle with chopped parsley, if you like, then gobble it up straight from the pan.

PRAWN AND BEANSPROUT OMELETTE

SERVES 1

This is my version of Egg Foo Yung, and it's a really quick breakfast option. Feel free to add other vegetables to the mix too.

INGREDIENTS

3 eggs
2 tsp light soy sauce
2 tsp toasted sesame oil
pepper
1 tbsp groundnut oil
200g cooked prawns
30g beansprouts
½ red chilli, finely sliced –
   remove the seeds if you
   don't like it hot
20g cashew nuts, roughly
   chopped
few leaves of coriander –
   optional

METHOD

Crack the eggs into a bowl and add the soy sauce and sesame oil, along with a grinding of black pepper. Beat together thoroughly.

Pour the groundnut oil into a small (about 15cm) non-stick frying pan over a high heat. When the oil is hot, pour the beaten egg mixture into the pan and use a wooden or plastic spoon to move the egg around as it cooks, a little like making scrambled eggs. When there is more firm egg than loose, turn the heat down to medium.

Lay the prawns on top of the omelette, followed by the beansprouts. Fold the omelette in half over the filling and let everything warm through for 30 seconds.

Gently tip your omelette onto a plate and top with the red chilli, cashew nuts and coriander leaves, if using.

POACHED SALMON WITH BACON

Mmm, bacon and salmon. Yes, please! This dish is a real winner on flavour, and it's full of those essential omega-3 fatty acids that will help to keep you lean.

MAKE AHEAD

INGREDIENTS

2 x 250g skinless salmon fillets

½ tbsp olive oil

2 rashers of thick smoked back bacon, trimmed of visible fat and sliced into 1cm strips

1 courgette, cut into half moons

200g midget trees (tender-stem broccoli), any bigger stalks sliced in half lengthways

8 cherry tomatoes

2 handfuls of baby spinach leaves

salt and pepper

40g pine nuts

finely grated parmesan, to serve

METHOD

Bring a large saucepan of water to the boil. Carefully slide the salmon fillets into the water and reduce the heat to just simmering. Poach the fish for 10 minutes or until just cooked through. Using a slotted spoon, carefully lift the fish out of the water and drain well.

While the fish is cooking, heat the oil in a large frying pan over a medium to high heat. When the oil is hot, fry the bacon for 1 minute, then add the courgette and midget trees and fry for another minute. Throw in the cherry tomatoes and cook for a further minute or until the tomatoes start to burst open and leak some of their delicious juices. Add the spinach and let it wilt down, then season with a little salt and a generous amount of pepper.

Divide the bacon and vegetable mixture between two plates, top with the poached salmon and finish with a scattering of pine nuts. Serve with a little finely grated parmesan.

SEA BASS WITH SPICED CAULIFLOWER, PEAS AND PANEER

SERVES 2

The Indian fresh cheese known as paneer is very similar to halloumi, and it goes perfectly with the sea bass and cauliflower in this dish. Feel free to use halloumi if you can't find paneer. Garam masala is a store cupboard essential and brings a big boost of flavour to almost anything!

INGREDIENTS

1 small cauliflower, broken into florets
1 tbsp coconut oil
1 red onion, diced
2cm ginger, finely chopped
150g paneer, roughly diced into 2cm cubes
1 tbsp garam masala
125g frozen peas
2 handfuls of baby spinach leaves
½ bunch of coriander, leaves only, roughly chopped
4 x 120g fillets of sea bass, skin on, but scaled
salt and pepper
juice of 1 lime

METHOD

Bring a large saucepan of water to the boil, then drop in the cauliflower florets and cook for 3 minutes. Drain in a sieve or colander, then rinse under cold running water. Leave the florets cooling in the sieve or colander.

In a large frying pan or wok, heat half the coconut oil over a medium to high heat. Add the onion and stir-fry for 2 minutes or until just starting to soften, then add the ginger and stir-fry for a further minute.

Add the paneer, garam masala and peas and keep stir-frying for 1–2 minutes, or until the peas have defrosted and are warmed through. If the garam masala seems to be catching on the bottom of the pan and burning, just add a drizzle of water. Chuck in the spinach, cauliflower and coriander and stir until the spinach has wilted.

In a separate frying pan, heat the rest of the coconut oil over a medium to high heat. Season the fish fillets with salt and pepper and, when the oil is hot, lay the fish in the pan, skin side down. Fry without turning for 1–2 minutes until the skin is crisp, then flip the fish over and cook for a final minute.

Divide the paneer and vegetables between two plates and top with the sea bass. Finish with a squeeze of lime juice.

CODDLED EGGS WITH SPINACH AND BACON

SERVES 1

Coddled eggs are basically steamed, creamy eggs. I love their texture, but if you would rather have poached or scrambled eggs, then go for it.

INGREDIENTS

large knob of butter
2 large eggs
½ tbsp olive oil
4 rashers of smoked back bacon, trimmed of visible fat and sliced into 1cm thick strips
2 large handfuls of baby spinach leaves
salt and pepper
2 tbsp pine nuts

METHOD

Bring a large saucepan of water to the boil and set a steamer basket on top.

Drop a chunk of butter into two ramekin dishes, then crack an egg into each one. When the water is boiling and there is a good amount of steam running through the steamer, carefully place the ramekins into the basket. Cover and steam the eggs for 6–10 minutes or until the whites are firm, but the yolks are still runny.

Meanwhile, heat the olive oil in a large frying pan over a medium to high heat. Add the bacon and fry for 1–2 minutes or until crisp. Stir in the spinach and cook until it has wilted, then season with salt and pepper.

Serve up the coddled eggs with the bacon and spinach, topped with a sprinkling of pine nuts.

**SERVES
2**

MAKE AHEAD

INGREDIENTS

4 tbsp light olive oil

2 x 250g skinless salmon
  fillets

1 tsp Dijon mustard

juice of ½ lemon

2 tsp capers

1 avocado, roughly diced

2 ripe tomatoes, roughly
  chopped

1 ball of mozzarella, torn
  into pieces

small handful of basil leaves

50g walnuts, roughly chopped

SALMON WITH CAPERS AND CAPRESE SALAD

Close your eyes when you eat this and you could be in Italy:
Caprese salad, capers and fresh basil. What a combo!

METHOD

Heat 1 tablespoon of the olive oil in a frying pan over a
medium to high heat. Add the salmon fillets and fry for
1–2 minutes on each side, by which time the fish should be
lightly coloured. Using a spatula, break the fish into large
chunks and fry for a further 2–3 minutes or until the fish
is just cooked through. Remove the pan from the heat and
transfer the salmon to a plate.

Mix together the mustard, lemon juice, capers and the
remaining olive oil to make a dressing.

Arrange the avocado, tomato and mozzarella over two
plates. Top with the salmon chunks, scatter with the basil
leaves and walnuts, and finally spoon over the dressing.

★ TOP TIP

Buy herb plants, sit them in a window box or on a
windowsill and you'll have free herbs forever.

TERIYAKI SALMON WITH COURGETTE NOODLES

SERVES 1

MAKE AHEAD
INGREDIENTS

½ tbsp coconut oil
1 x 240g skinless salmon
   fillet
2 spring onions, finely sliced
2cm ginger, finely chopped
2 tbsp light soy sauce
1 tbsp honey
½ tbsp rice wine vinegar
4 cherry tomatoes, cut in half
1 large courgette, spiralized
   or sliced to make long
   noodle-like strands
2 tsp sesame oil

If you don't have a spiralizer, make the courgette noodles by using a peeler to create long thin ribbons of courgette, which you can then stack up and slice with a knife into noodle-like strips.

METHOD

Heat half of the coconut oil in a frying pan over a medium to high heat. When the oil is melted and hot, slide in the salmon and fry for 2–3 minutes on each side or until lightly browned and almost cooked through.

Meanwhile, mix together the spring onions, ginger, soy sauce, honey and vinegar to make a teriyaki sauce. Pour this into the pan with the salmon and let it bubble up, then remove the pan from the heat.

In another frying pan, heat the remaining coconut oil over a high heat. Tumble in the tomatoes and stir-fry for 1 minute. Gently add the courgette noodles and lightly toss for 1 minute just to warm through.

Plate up the noodles and tomatoes, then top with the teriyaki salmon. Finish with a little drizzle of sesame oil.

MAKE AHEAD
(but reheat in the oven,
not in the microwave)
GOOD TO FREEZE
INGREDIENTS

50g rolled oats
50g ground almonds
3 tsp smoked paprika
salt and pepper
1 egg
2 x 220g skinless chicken
  breast fillets
2 tbsp plain flour
1 tbsp coconut oil
½ cucumber, roughly
  chopped into 2cm pieces
1 large tomato, roughly
  chopped
1 avocado, roughly chopped
1 tbsp olive oil
squeeze of lemon juice

MY OATY CHICKEN

Feeling stressed out after a long day at work? Cook this meal and you can take it out on your chicken, as you get to give it a good bash with a rolling pin or your fists to make it cook more quickly. Oh, and did I mention it's covered in an oaty, nutty crispy coating that tastes out of this world when you fry it in coconut oil?

METHOD

In a shallow dish, mix together the rolled oats, ground almonds, smoked paprika and a generous pinch of salt and pepper. Crack the egg into another shallow bowl and whisk.

Lay a large sheet of cling film on your chopping board and place the chicken breasts on it, allowing room for them to spread, then place another sheet of cling film on top. Using a rolling pin, meat hammer or other blunt instrument, bash the breasts until they are half their original thickness and flattened out. Remove the chicken breasts from the cling film and dust all over with the flour, shaking them lightly to remove any excess, then dip into the beaten egg, again shaking off any excess. Finally, dunk the chicken breasts into the oat and almond mixture, pressing it on to cover both sides as well as you can.

Heat the coconut oil in a large non-stick frying pan over a medium heat. Carefully lay the chicken breasts into the oil and fry for about 4 minutes on each side or until the chicken is cooked through. Check by cutting into the thickest part to make sure the meat is white, with no signs of pink. Transfer the chicken to paper towels to drain off any excess oil.

Mix together the cucumber, tomato, avocado, olive oil and lemon juice to make a quick salad, then serve alongside the oaty chicken.

MUSSELS IN COCONUT MILK

SERVES 2

If you've never tried mussels cooked in coconut milk, you're in for a treat. They make a nice change from fish or prawns, and they taste great.

INGREDIENTS

1 tbsp coconut oil

2 star anise

6 spring onions, finely sliced

2 cloves garlic, finely chopped

1 lemongrass stalk, bruised with the back of a knife

1 red chilli, roughly chopped – remove the seeds if you don't like it hot

1 x 400ml tin of full-fat coconut milk

2kg mussels, shells scrubbed and beards removed

2 tbsp fish sauce

small bunch of coriander, leaves only, roughly chopped

2 limes

METHOD

Heat the coconut oil in a very large pan or wok for which you have a lid (or you can improvise with a large dinner plate or a sheet of foil). When the oil has melted, add the star anise, spring onions, garlic, lemongrass and chilli and stir-fry for 1 minute or until the spring onions and garlic are starting to soften – by now the smell should be getting your appetite going too!

Pour in the coconut milk and bring to the boil, then reduce the heat and simmer for about 3 minutes to reduce the liquid a little. Check your mussels at this point: if there are any that are open and do not clamp shut when tapped, throw them away. Tumble the mussels into the coconut milk and give them a stir, then cover and cook for 3–4 minutes, shaking the pan every now and then. The mussels are cooked when their shells are fully open – be careful not to overcook, as that's how they become chewy. Discard any mussels that don't open up.

Remove the pan from the heat and stir in the fish sauce, half of the chopped coriander and the juice of one of the limes. Divide the mussels between two bowls and garnish with the rest of the coriander. Cut the other lime in half and serve on the side of the bowl, for squeezing.

★ Serve with a big portion of your favourite greens such as spinach, kale, broccoli, mange tout or green beans.

STEAK WITH SPICY CHORIZO, TOMATOES AND KALE

Ooh, steak and chorizo in one dish? Count me in! This is a real meat lover's dish. If you're not a fan of kale, you could always use spinach, but be sure to get your greens in.

INGREDIENTS

2 tbsp olive oil
2 x 240g sirloin steaks, trimmed of visible fat
salt and pepper
75g cured chorizo, diced
200g kale, thick stalks removed
8 cherry tomatoes, cut in half
1 tbsp sherry vinegar, or balsamic or red wine vinegar

METHOD

Bring a large saucepan of water to the boil, and place a frying pan over a high heat.

Rub the olive oil all over the steaks and season generously with salt and pepper. When the pan is very hot, carefully lay the steaks in it and fry for 2 minutes before flipping and frying for another 2 minutes. Transfer the steak to a plate and leave to rest.

Meanwhile, throw the chorizo into the same frying pan, turn the heat down to low and cook for about 2 minutes. At the same time, drop the kale into the boiling water and simmer for 1 minute, then drain in a sieve or colander.

Crank up the heat under the chorizo to maximum, then add the tomatoes to the pan and stir-fry for 1 minute. Pour in the vinegar and let it bubble away to almost nothing. Add the kale and toss to combine everything thoroughly.

Remove from the heat and season to taste with salt and pepper. Place a steak on each plate and top with the delicious stir-fry.

CLASSIC SMOKED SALMON AND SCRAMBLED EGGS

SERVES 2

The king of healthy breakfasts is a true Lean in 15 dish!
If you're always in a rush in the morning, this one's for you.
Scrambling the eggs on a low heat with butter gives them
a seriously creamy texture.

INGREDIENTS

6 eggs
20g butter, roughly chopped
pepper
6 slices smoked salmon,
 cut into 1cm thick strips
small bunch of chives,
 finely sliced
handful of baby spinach
 leaves, to serve

METHOD

Bring a saucepan of water to the boil.

Crack the eggs into a large heatproof bowl and add the
butter, along with a good grinding of pepper. Whisk the eggs
together, then sit the bowl over the pan of boiling water and
immediately reduce the heat to a simmer. Cook the eggs
for about 10 minutes, stirring regularly. As the eggs begin to
scramble, add the smoked salmon and the chives, and keep
cooking the eggs until they reach your preferred consistency –
the longer you cook them, the firmer they'll get.

Serve up these luxurious eggs with a big handful of spinach
and a final grinding of black pepper.

SEA BASS WITH BRAZIL NUTS, KALE AND POMEGRANATE

SERVES 1

Sea bass with nuts and pomegranate – such a great combination of flavours and packed with goodness. This is a dish to impress your friends at a dinner party!

MAKE AHEAD

INGREDIENTS

2 tbsp olive oil
2 x 120g sea bass fillets, skin on
salt and pepper
75g kale, thick stalks removed
4 midget trees (tender-stem broccoli), any bigger stalks sliced in half lengthways
2 tbsp pomegranate seeds
25g brazil nuts, chopped
1 red chilli, finely sliced – remove the seeds if you don't like it hot

METHOD

Bring a saucepan of water to the boil.

Meanwhile, heat half of the olive oil in a frying pan over a medium to high heat. Season the sea bass with salt and pepper and, when the oil is hot, carefully lay the fish in the pan, skin side down. Cook, without turning, for 2–3 minutes, then carefully flip it over. Remove the pan from the heat and let the fish finish cooking in the residual heat.

Drop the kale and midget trees into the boiling water and simmer for 2 minutes. Drain in a sieve or colander, then rinse under cold running water. Transfer the vegetables to a bowl and add the rest of the olive oil, along with the pomegranate seeds, brazil nuts and chilli. Gently toss everything together.

Pile the vegetables onto the plate, sit the fish on top, and tuck in.

GRIDDLED MIDGET TREES AND SPEARS WITH EGGS

SERVES 2

What can I say? You know how obsessed I am with midget trees! Well, here's a breakfast idea I'm sure you'll love as much as I do.

INGREDIENTS

8 spears of asparagus, woody parts of stalks removed
8 midget trees (tender-stem broccoli)
2 rashers of smoked back bacon
salt and pepper
150g pre-cooked puy lentils
4 eggs
glug of olive oil
splash of sherry vinegar
2 tbsp toasted and chopped hazelnuts

METHOD

Bring a large saucepan of water to the boil and place a griddle pan over a high heat. It's probably best to throw open a window too, as griddling always seems to set the smoke alarm off . . .

When the griddle pan is hot, place the spears, trees and bacon directly onto it, sprinkling the vegetables with a little salt and pepper. Cook for 3–4 minutes, turning regularly – you're after crispy bacon and lightly chargrilled vegetables.

Ping the lentils in the microwave according to the packet instructions.

Carefully crack your eggs into the hot water, reducing the heat until the water is just 'burping'. Cook the eggs for about 4 minutes for a runny yolk, then carefully lift them out with a slotted spoon and drain on paper towels.

Once the veg are all cooked, scoop them up and drop them into a large bowl. Remove the bacon and roughly chop, then add to the bowl too, along with the olive oil, sherry vinegar and lentils. Season to taste with salt and pepper and toss the whole lot together before piling onto plates. Top with the poached eggs and finish with the toasted hazelnuts.

SERVES 1

MAKE AHEAD

INGREDIENTS

1 tbsp olive oil
240g duck breast fillet, sliced
  into 2cm thick strips
salt and pepper
100g green beans
1 tbsp walnut oil
40g walnuts
2 tbsp sundried tomatoes

DUCK, GREEN BEANS AND WALNUTS

Oh, hello, healthy fats! Although this feels like a high-end bistro dish, it's ready in minutes. And as it's just as tasty eaten at room temperature, it works very well as a packed lunch too.

METHOD

Bring a large saucepan of water to the boil.

Heat the olive oil in a frying pan over a medium to high heat. Season the duck breast with salt and pepper. When the oil is hot, add the duck and fry, stirring occasionally, for about 3 minutes or until the duck is cooked through and lightly golden in places.

Meanwhile, drop the beans into the boiling water and simmer for 1 minute. Drain in a sieve or colander, then rinse under cold running water. Tip the beans into a bowl and add the walnut oil, walnuts and sundried tomatoes. Season generously with salt and pepper, then toss everything together.

Arrange the green beans and walnuts on a plate and top with the duck.

MAKE AHEAD
GOOD TO FREEZE

INGREDIENTS

½ tbsp coconut oil
½ red onion, diced
1 red or yellow pepper,
 de-seeded and thinly sliced
½ courgette, diced
300g ready-made turkey
 meatballs (available at
 most supermarkets)
1 x 400g tin of chopped
 tomatoes
20g feta, crumbled
½ bunch of parsley, leaves
only, roughly chopped –
 optional

TURKEY MEATBALLS WITH FETA

These meatballs went down a treat on Instagram, ranking as one of my most popular videos. The cheesy sauce also tastes great with beef meatballs. Feel free to throw in any extra veg you have left in the fridge too.

METHOD

Heat the coconut oil in a large frying pan over a medium to high heat. Add the onion, pepper and courgette, and stir-fry for 2 minutes until the vegetables begin to soften and wilt.

Increase the heat to maximum and roll the meatballs into the pan. Fry for 2–3 minutes, moving them frequently so they brown all over.

Pour in the chopped tomatoes and bring to the boil, then reduce the heat and simmer for 5 minutes, or until the meatballs are fully cooked through. To check, cut the largest one in half and make sure all the meat has turned from pink to white.

Remove the pan from the heat, crumble over the feta and sprinkle with parsley, if using.

★ **TOP TIP**

If you can't find ready-made turkey meatballs in your supermarket, simply buy turkey mince and season it with a generous amount of salt and pepper. Create some extra flavour by adding in a pinch of dried oregano, parsley or Cajun spice. Knead for a minute and then form into golfball-sized meatballs.

LAMB KOFTAS WITH GREEK SALAD

This is a great summer dish and is brilliant on a barbecue. The fresh crispness of the salad cuts through the richness of the meat. If you want to change it up, beef mince works well with this recipe too.

MAKE AHEAD
GOOD TO FREEZE
(the koftas, not the salad!)

INGREDIENTS

350g lean lamb mince
2 tsp ground cinnamon
2 tsp ground cumin
4 spring onions, finely sliced
2 cloves garlic, finely chopped
salt and pepper
½ cucumber, roughly
  chopped into big chunks
1 large tomato, roughly
  chopped into big chunks
16 black olives
splash of sherry vinegar
small handful of mint leaves,
  to serve – optional

METHOD

Preheat your grill to maximum.

Tip the lamb mince into a bowl. Add the cinnamon and cumin, spring onions, garlic and a generous pinch of salt and pepper, then mix the whole lot together thoroughly – I find the best way is to dig your hands in there.

Mould the mince mixture into 4 equal-sized sausage shapes around a skewer and place on your grill pan or a baking tray. Grill the koftas for 5 minutes on each side or until well browned and cooked through.

Meanwhile, toss the cucumber, tomato, olives and vinegar together in a bowl.

Serve your koftas with this chunky salad – and an artistic scattering of mint leaves, if you like.

COCONUT AND CASHEW DAAL

A lovely vegetarian option to try. This is going to take rather longer than most of my recipes (about an hour for this one), but it's time well spent, as it tastes amazing.

INGREDIENTS

250g yellow split peas
  (available in most
  supermarkets)
1 tbsp coconut oil
1 small red onion, roughly
  diced
1 tsp cumin seeds
1 cinnamon stick, broken
  in two
1 fresh bay leaf, or 2 dried
4 cloves garlic, finely chopped
5cm ginger, finely chopped
1 green chilli, split lengthways
1 tbsp garam masala
1 tsp ground turmeric
1 x 400ml tin of full-fat
  coconut milk
500ml warm vegetable stock
200g cashew nuts
2 large handfuls of baby
  spinach leaves
bunch of coriander, leaves
  only, roughly chopped

METHOD

Place the split peas in a large bowl and cover with warm water from the tap. Leave to soak while you cook the onion and spices.

Melt the coconut oil in a large saucepan over a medium heat. Add the onion and cook for 3–4 minutes until just soft. Add the cumin seeds, cinnamon and bay leaves and stir-fry for 45 seconds, then add the garlic, ginger and chilli and cook for 1 minute. Sprinkle in the garam masala and turmeric powder and stir-fry for 30 seconds.

Drain the split peas and add to the pan, along with the coconut milk and half of the vegetable stock. Bring to the boil and simmer for about 30 minutes or until the split peas are completely tender.

Meanwhile, pour the rest of the vegetable stock over the cashew nuts and leave to soak for 10 minutes. Tip the nuts and stock into a blender and blitz until smooth.

When the split peas are tender, add the cashew cream and the spinach, then stir until the spinach has wilted into the daal. Remove from the heat and stir through the coriander before gobbling down your yummy daal.

★ Serve with a big portion of your favourite greens such as spinach, kale, broccoli, mange tout or green beans.

LONGER RECIPE
MAKE AHEAD
GOOD TO FREEZE

INGREDIENTS

3 aubergines, cut lengthways
  into slices about 5mm thick
about 100ml olive oil
salt and pepper
1 large red onion, diced
3 cloves garlic, finely chopped
1kg turkey mince
1 tsp ground cinnamon
1 tbsp tomato puree
300ml chicken stock
2 tsp dried oregano
2 balls of mozzarella (about
  250g)
4 tbsp finely grated parmesan
bunch of parsley, leaves
  only, roughly chopped

TURKEY MOUSSAKA

Grilled aubergine is hard to beat – and in this moussaka, it becomes perfect dinner-party fodder. Even better, it can all be done in advance, so it's fuss-free. This dish actually takes more like 1 hour and 15 minutes to make, but for much of that time it looks after itself in the oven.

METHOD

Preheat your grill to maximum. Lay a single layer of aubergine slices on your grill pan or a baking tray, drizzle with a little olive oil and season with salt and pepper. Slide under the grill and cook for 2 minutes on each side. When cooked (soft to the touch and looking a little shrivelled), transfer the aubergine slices to a plate and repeat the process until they are all cooked and sitting happily on the plate.

Heat a splash of olive oil in a large saucepan over a medium to high heat. Add the onion and garlic and stir-fry for 3–4 minutes until beginning to soften. Increase the heat to high and add the turkey mince, cinnamon, tomato puree, chicken stock and oregano. Bring the whole lot up to the boil and leave to simmer for 20 minutes.

Preheat your oven to 190°C (fan 170°C, gas mark 5).

Pour about a quarter of the mince mixture into a deep baking dish. Tear up half a ball of mozzarella and scatter over the mince, then lay a third of the grilled aubergine slices on top (it doesn't matter if they overlap slightly). Repeat the process until you have 3 layers of mince and 3 layers of aubergine, then finish with the final quarter of the mince.

Scatter the parmesan over the top and cook the moussaka in the oven for about 30 minutes until heated through and golden brown. To finish your dish, sprinkle over the fresh parsley.

JOE'S CHICKEN PIE

If you love chicken pie, this recipe won't disappoint. It's actually Lean in about 60 minutes, but is such a nice treat that you won't mind the extra effort. Plus, there's cream and butter in it, so you know it's going to taste incredible.

LONGER RECIPE
MAKE AHEAD
GOOD TO FREEZE

INGREDIENTS

2 large knobs of butter
1 large leek, washed and
  chopped into 2cm pieces
200g mushrooms, roughly
  chopped
4 x 250g chicken breast fillets,
  cut into bite-sized pieces
250ml chicken stock
1 tbsp cornflour
100ml double cream
2 large handfuls of baby
  spinach leaves
about 6 sheets of filo pastry
drizzle of olive oil
salad or veg, to serve

METHOD

Preheat your oven to 190°C (fan 170°C, gas mark 5).

Heat the butter in a large frying pan over a medium to high heat. Add the leek and mushrooms and fry for 2–3 minutes until they just start to soften. Crank up the heat to high, add the chicken pieces and fry for a further 2 minutes – the chicken won't be cooked through at this point – then pour in the chicken stock and let it come to a simmer.

Meanwhile, mix the cornflour with 2 tablespoons of water until smooth, then pour into the pan, along with the cream. Bring back to the boil, stirring gently, and cook until the sauce thickens. Remove from the heat and stir in the spinach, then tip the whole lot into a pie dish about 28cm x 15cm. Set aside to cool a little.

Take a sheet of filo and roughly crumple it in your hands – there is no right or wrong to this method! Place the crumpled filo on top of the chicken filling in the pie dish and repeat with the remaining filo sheets.

Drizzle the pastry with olive oil, then bake the pie for about 20 minutes, by which time the filo will have crisped up and turned golden brown in places.

Serve up your pie with fresh salad or some vegetables.

POST-WORKOUT CARBOHYDRATE-REFUEL RECIPES

4

BANANA AND BLUEBERRY OVERNIGHT OATS

SERVES 1

This is a quick and easy breakfast to have ready to go, after jump-starting your day with a morning workout.

INGREDIENTS

1 banana, roughly chopped
75g full-fat yoghurt
250ml almond milk
1 scoop (30g) strawberry
  protein powder
100g rolled oats
handful of pistachios or
  other nuts, blueberries and
  raspberries to serve

METHOD

Place the banana, yoghurt, almond milk and protein powder into a blender and blend until smooth. Pour the mixture into a bowl and stir in the oats, then cover and refrigerate for at least 4 hours, preferably overnight.

When ready to eat, top with the nuts, blueberries and raspberries.

BIG McLEAN MUFFIN

SERVES 1

The thought of one of these waiting for you once you've finished your workout is enough to get you through those last reps. For the best poached eggs, use the freshest eggs possible.

INGREDIENTS

- 2 eggs
- 2 tsp coconut oil
- 5 cherry tomatoes
- 2 massive handfuls of baby spinach leaves
- 1 large English muffin
- 240g deli-style sliced ham or gammon, trimmed of visible fat
- 1 red chilli, finely sliced – optional

METHOD

Bring a saucepan of water to the boil. Carefully crack your eggs into the hot water, reducing the heat until the water is just 'burping'. Cook the eggs for about 4 minutes for runny yolks, then carefully lift them out with a slotted spoon and drain on paper towels.

Meanwhile, heat the coconut oil in a large frying pan over a medium to high heat. Add the tomatoes and toss in the hot oil for 1–2 minutes or until they are lightly browned and blistered. At this point, throw in the spinach and toss with the tomatoes until wilted, then remove the pan from the heat.

Toast your muffin, top with the ham or gammon and spoon over the tomatoes and spinach, then finish with the poached eggs and some sliced red chilli, if using.

WINNER'S PROTEIN PANCAKES

SERVES 1

Oooh, I can eat pancakes and get lean? Yes please – sold! These may look naughty, but they're actually the perfect post-workout treat, so stack 'em up and enjoy. You've earned them!

INGREDIENTS

1 banana, roughly chopped
1 scoop (30g) vanilla protein powder
1 egg
25g rolled oats
1 tbsp coconut oil
full-fat Greek yoghurt, blueberries and raspberries, to serve

METHOD

Whizz up the banana, protein powder, egg and oats in a blender to make your batter.

Heat up half the coconut oil in a non-stick frying pan over a medium heat. Pour little puddles of batter into the pan – I usually get 3 pancakes, with about half the batter in the pan at once. Cook for about 1 minute on each side. Remove and repeat the process with the rest of the batter.

Serve with a dollop of yoghurt and a few berries (see picture overleaf).

INGREDIENTS

75g rolled oats
large handful of blueberries
handful of ice cubes
1 banana, roughly chopped
1 scoop (30g) vanilla or
   strawberry protein powder
1 tbsp chia seeds
250ml coconut water or water

BLUEBERRY AND BANANA PROTEIN SHAKE

This is a great way to get a load of vitamins into your diet, as it's so easy to make and transport (you can have it on your morning commute). I really recommend a good blender: they're worth their weight in gold. Just remember that protein shakes are fine to have now and then, but they aren't meant to replace actual food – so keep mixing it up!

METHOD

Place all the ingredients in a blender and blend until smooth.

★ TOP TIP

Chia seeds were an important food for the Aztecs and Mayans back in the day. They prized them for their ability to provide sustainable energy – in fact, 'chia' is the ancient Mayan word for 'strength'. Don't be fooled by their size! As a good source of fibre, protein and antioxidants, these little seeds pack a nutritional power punch.

INGREDIENTS

200ml almond milk
1 granny smith apple, cored
   and roughly chopped
2 large handfuls (120g) of
   baby spinach leaves
1 scoop (30g) vanilla protein
   powder
75g rolled oats

INCREDIBLE HULK SMOOTHIE

This is green and good for you. I like to leave the skin on my apple, as it is full of nutrients, but you may prefer not to – either way is fine! Enjoy.

METHOD

Place all the ingredients in a blender with a handful of ice and blitz until smooth.

BUILD-UP BAGEL

Long live the build-up bagel. For some reason, people on my plan go absolutely bonkers for this post-workout bagel. I think they feel naughty eating it – but, like I say, you've just trained and earned those carbs, so no need to feel guilty. Go for good-quality cooked meat, not the nasty cheap re-formed stuff. If you don't want to bother with poaching the egg, you could always just boil and slice it instead.

**SERVES
1**

INGREDIENTS

1 egg
1 plain bagel
2 tsp chipotle paste or
  barbecue sauce
1 tbsp full-fat Greek yoghurt
large handful of rocket
1 tomato, sliced
150g deli-style cooked turkey
  or chicken breast
75g deli-style sliced roast beef

METHOD

Bring a saucepan of water to the boil. Carefully crack your egg into the hot water, reducing the heat until the water is just 'burping'. Cook the egg for about 4 minutes for a runny yolk, then carefully lift it out with a slotted spoon and drain on paper towels.

Slice the bagel in half and toast it for a couple of minutes.

Spread the toasted bagel evenly with the chipotle paste or barbecue sauce and the yoghurt, and then begin building your bagel: start with the rocket and tomato, followed by the turkey or chicken and the beef, then the poached egg. Finally, stick the top on the bagel and get munching!

CHICKEN AND NEW POTATO HASH

SERVES 1

Standing around waiting for potatoes to boil? No, thanks. Bang them in the microwave instead and cook them in half the time. This is proper comfort food – a real reward after a workout. You won't feel hungry after this one.

INGREDIENTS

200g new potatoes
½ tbsp coconut oil
1 x 200g skinless chicken breast fillet, sliced into 1cm thick strips
4 spring onions, sliced
75g mange tout
1 egg
1 tsp smoked paprika
2 large handfuls of baby spinach leaves
pinch of chilli flakes, if you like it hot

METHOD

Prick the new potatoes with a fork and blast them in the microwave at 900w for 8 minutes.

Meanwhile, melt the oil in a large frying pan over a medium to high heat. Add the chicken and fry for 2 minutes, stirring occasionally – you want the chicken to be browned in places. Add the spring onions and the mange tout and stir-fry for 1 minute, then remove from the heat. You should now have about 4 minutes until your spuds ping, so time for a quick set of press-ups – go!

Bring a saucepan of water to the boil. Carefully crack your egg into the hot water, reducing the heat until the water is just 'burping'. Cook the egg for about 4 minutes for a runny yolk, then carefully lift it out with a slotted spoon and drain on paper towels.

Once the spuds have pinged, carefully (maybe using a knife and fork, as they'll be very hot) halve them, cutting any larger ones into quarters. Return the frying pan to a high heat, then slide in the potatoes and fry, without turning, for about 3–4 minutes or until the potatoes are beginning to brown in places. Add the smoked paprika and spinach, then toss to coat all the ingredients evenly and wilt the spinach.

Spoon up your hash, top with the poached egg and finish with a little chilli flake fire, if you want.

MAKE AHEAD

INGREDIENTS

1 tbsp coconut oil

500g sirloin steak, trimmed of visible fat and cut into 1cm thick slices

1 red onion, roughly chopped

1 red pepper, de-seeded and roughly sliced

1 clove garlic, finely chopped

1 tsp paprika

1 tsp dried oregano

6 cherry tomatoes, roughly chopped

salt and pepper

1 x 400g tin of kidney beans, drained and rinsed

2 large tortilla wraps

small bunch of coriander, leaves only, roughly chopped

squeeze of lime juice

BAD-BOY BURRITO

You've just worked out and earned your carbs. This monster burrito needs two hands to eat, and is a proper treat that's guaranteed to fill you up and leave you feeling like a hero. It's also really quick and easy to make up and then carry with you to work. For a change, try using chicken instead of beef, or pitta bread instead of tortillas.

METHOD

Heat the coconut oil in a large frying pan over a high heat. Add the steak and fry for 1–2 minutes, turning the meat a couple of times. Throw in the onion, red pepper and garlic and stir-fry for a minute or two. Add the paprika, oregano and tomatoes, season with salt and pepper, and toss everything together for a minute. Chuck in the kidney beans and cook for another minute, by which time the beans should be warmed through.

Pile half the mixture along the middle of each wrap, then top with some chopped coriander and finish with a squeeze of lime juice. Roll up and gobble down.

**SERVES
1**

MAKE AHEAD
(the chilli not the sweet
potato)

INGREDIENTS

1 sweet potato
2 tsp coconut oil
3 spring onions, finely sliced
250g reduced-fat (about 5%)
  beef mince
1 tsp ground cumin
1 tsp smoked paprika
2 tsp tomato puree
175g tinned kidney beans,
  drained and rinsed
100ml beef stock
1 tbsp full-fat Greek yoghurt

SWEET POTATO WITH CHILLI

Sweet potato is one of my favourite carb sources and when you combine it with a quick beef chilli, it's a real banger. To make this Lean in 15, I use a microwave to cook the potato, but if you'd rather boil the sweet potato or bake it in the oven, go for it.

METHOD

Prick the sweet potato a couple of times with a fork, then blast it in the microwave at 900w for 5 minutes. Leave it to rest for 30 seconds and then blast it for a further 3–4 minutes. Set aside, loosely covered in foil, until needed.

Meanwhile, melt the coconut oil in a large frying pan over a high heat. Stir in the spring onions and beef and stir-fry for about 4 minutes, breaking up any chunks of mince as you go. When the meat is browned, sprinkle in the cumin and paprika and cook for 30 seconds before squeezing in the tomato puree. Stir-fry for another 30 seconds, then add the kidney beans and beef stock. Bring to a simmer and cook for 1 minute.

Split open the sweet potato and serve with the quick chilli – and some cooling yoghurt.

★ Serve with a big portion of your favourite greens such as spinach, kale, broccoli, mange tout or green beans.

PRAWN AND NOODLE STIR-FRY

This is about as lean as they come. One wok, no hassle and another chance to throw some midget trees around. This makes a great lunch, too, so cook double and take the extra in a lunch box to work the next day.

MAKE AHEAD
INGREDIENTS

½ tbsp coconut oil
3 spring onions, finely sliced
1 clove garlic, finely chopped
200g raw prawns, peeled
50g mange tout, sliced in half
3 baby sweetcorn, sliced in half
4 midget trees (tender-stem broccoli), any bigger stalks sliced in half lengthways
200g 'straight to wok' noodles
2 tbsp light soy sauce
1 tbsp fish sauce

METHOD

Melt the coconut oil in a wok or large frying pan over a medium to high heat. Add the spring onions and garlic and stir-fry for 1 minute. Add the prawns and continue to stir for a further minute.

Toss in the mange tout, sweetcorn and midget trees, along with about 2 tablespoons of water. Let the water bubble up and create steam to cook the vegetables. Add the noodles, breaking up the clumps with your fingers as you drop them in. Toss to mix the noodles with the other ingredients, then stir-fry for a minute until the noodles are warmed through and soft.

Remove from the heat, pour in the soy sauce and fish sauce, then give the whole lot one last stir before piling onto a plate and munching away.

★ TOP TIP

For a gluten-free meal, swap the soy sauce for tamari, and use rice noodles instead of the 'straight to wok' variety.

SERVES 1

IN-A-HURRY CURRY FRIED RICE

If you're craving a curry and thinking of ordering a greasy takeaway, hold your horses and make this instead. It's lean, it tastes great and it will arrive quicker than any Indian takeaway. It tastes awesome with diced pork or turkey too.

MAKE AHEAD
INGREDIENTS

1 tbsp coconut oil
1 small red onion, roughly diced
1 clove garlic, roughly diced
2cm ginger, roughly diced
250g skinless chicken breast fillet, sliced into 1cm thick strips
½ red pepper, de-seeded and sliced
1 tbsp mild curry powder
250g pre-cooked basmati rice
big handful of baby spinach leaves
squeeze of lime juice

METHOD

Melt the coconut oil in a wok or large frying pan over a medium to high heat. Add the onion and stir-fry for 1 minute, then add the garlic and ginger and cook for a further minute. Toss in the chicken, red pepper and half of the curry powder and stir-fry for 2 minutes.

Add the rice, crumbling it between your fingers as you drop it in, then pour in 2 tablespoons of water. Stir-fry for 2 minutes until the rice is warmed through and the chicken is completely cooked. Check by slicing into one of the larger pieces to make sure the meat is white all the way through, with no raw pink bits left.

Add the remaining curry powder, along with the spinach, and stir until the spinach has wilted slightly and the curry powder is evenly distributed.

Dish up your yummy curry fried rice, finishing with a big squeeze of lime juice.

THE BODY COACH CLUB SANDWICH

The Body Coach club sandwich is a beautiful thing! I've stuck with tradition and gone with turkey and ham, but feel free to improvise. And if the four-layer sandwich is too much for you, drop a layer and add a handful of sweet potato chips instead (see below).

MAKE AHEAD

INGREDIENTS

2 eggs
salt and pepper
4 slices of thick sliced bread
1 large tomato, sliced
½ round lettuce, leaves only
300g mixed sliced deli-style meats – I like turkey and ham
1 big pickled gherkin, to serve – optional

METHOD

Bring a saucepan of water to the boil before carefully lowering in the eggs and boiling for 6 minutes. Drain, then run the eggs under cold water until cool enough to handle and peel them. Place the eggs in a small bowl, season generously with salt and pepper, then crush with the back of a fork.

Toast your bread. When the toast is ready, build up your sandwich: lay the 4 slices of toast in front of you, spread each one with the crushed egg, then divide the tomato, lettuce and meat evenly among 3 of the slices. Stack up these 3 slices, then flip the last one over to create a lid.

Slice into triangles and gobble down with a gherkin chaser.

★ TOP TIP

To make the sweet potato chips, slice a large sweet potato lengthways into 8 wedges. Microwave the wedges for 4 minutes at 900w, then leave to stand for 1 minute. Heat 1 tbsp of coconut oil and fry the par-cooked chips in the oil until brown and crisp all over. Drain on paper towels and season with salt.

THAI BEEF STIR-FRY

SERVES 1

Fast and full of vibrant flavours, this will become a favourite. I predict you'll be eating this once a week when you've tried it. And if you become bored with egg noodles, try any of the 'straight to wok' types, or choose rice noodles for a gluten-free meal.

MAKE AHEAD

INGREDIENTS

½ tbsp coconut oil
2 star anise
1 bird's eye chilli, finely
  chopped – remove the seeds
  if you don't like it hot
2 cloves garlic, finely chopped
3 spring onions, finely sliced
1 lemongrass stalk, tender
  white part only, finely sliced
250g sirloin steak, trimmed
  of visible fat and sliced into
  1cm thick strips
240g fresh egg noodles
2 tsp fish sauce
small bunch of coriander,
  leaves only, roughly chopped
juice of 1 lime

METHOD

Melt the coconut oil in a wok or large frying pan over a high heat. Add the star anise and leave to infuse the oil for 30 seconds, then remove. Add the chilli, garlic, spring onions and lemongrass and stir-fry for 1 minute.

Add the steak and stir-fry for a further 1–2 minutes until the beef is almost cooked.

Tumble in the noodles, along with a couple of tablespoons of water – this will create steam, helping to separate and warm the egg noodles. Toss everything together until you are satisfied that the beef is cooked and the noodles are warmed through.

Remove from the heat, add the fish sauce, coriander and lime juice, then serve up.

BAHN MI (VIETNAMESE PORK SANDWICH)

This Vietnamese speciality uses pork loin, which is a great source of low-fat, inexpensive protein.

SERVES 1

MAKE AHEAD

INGREDIENTS

½ tbsp coconut oil
½ red onion, sliced into thin
  wedges
300g pork fillet, cut into 1cm
  thick slices
1 red chilli, sliced – remove
  the seeds if you don't like
  it hot
3 tsp fish sauce
juice of 2 limes
2 tsp honey
2 tsp sesame oil
½ large baguette
1 tbsp chipotle paste
1 baby gem lettuce, leaves
  separated
¼ cucumber, sliced into thin
  batons
mint and coriander leaves,
  to serve

METHOD

Melt the coconut oil in a wok or frying pan over a medium to high heat. Add the onion and fry for 2 minutes or until starting to soften. Increase the heat to high, add the pork and chilli and stir-fry for 2–3 minutes, by which time the pork should be cooked through. Check by cutting into one of the larger pieces of meat to make sure there is no pink left. Remove the pan from the heat and pour in the fish sauce, lime juice, honey and sesame oil. Toss everything together until well mixed.

Cut the baguette in half lengthways and spread evenly with the chipotle paste. Build up your sandwich by laying lettuce leaves on the base, followed by the pork, cucumber and fresh herbs. Clamp the other half of the baguette on top and devour it.

SAG ALOO WITH CHICKEN

Potatoes don't need to be bland and boring. This Indian-inspired dish tastes incredible and is much leaner than a greasy takeaway from your local curry house.

MAKE AHEAD

INGREDIENTS

250g new potatoes
½ tbsp coconut oil
4 spring onions, finely sliced
2 cloves garlic, finely chopped
2cm ginger, finely chopped
1 tbsp garam masala
1 x 240g skinless chicken
  breast fillet, sliced into 1cm
  thick strips
salt and pepper
2 large handfuls of baby
  spinach leaves
½ bunch of coriander, leaves
  only, roughly chopped
squeeze of lemon juice

METHOD

Prick each potato once with a fork. Place in a microwave-proof bowl, pour over a splash of water and microwave for 2½ minutes at 900w, then leave to rest for 30 seconds before giving them a final 3-minute blast. Leave the potatoes to stand for a further 30 seconds, before carefully slicing them in half.

Melt the coconut oil in a wok or large frying pan over a medium to high heat. Add the spring onions, garlic and ginger and fry for 1 minute, stirring regularly. Tumble in the potatoes and mix in well. Sprinkle in the garam masala and fry for 30 seconds, stirring constantly – be careful not to let it catch. Quickly add the chicken, along with 2 tablespoons of water, to help cook the chicken and stop the spices burning. Season generously with salt and pepper and fry for 3–4 minutes, by which time the chicken should be cooked through. Check by slicing into one of the larger pieces to make sure the meat is white all the way through, with no raw pink bits left.

Add the spinach and toss through until wilted – there is no such thing as too much spinach at this point! Remove from the heat, sprinkle in the coriander and finish with a squeeze of lemon juice.

TURKEY AND CHICKPEA PITTAS

The flavours in this dish remind me of falafel. If you don't have chickpeas, try making it with cannellini or butter beans. And, if you like, you can ditch the pitta and wrap it all up in a tortilla instead!

MAKE AHEAD

INGREDIENTS

200g tinned chickpeas, drained and rinsed
½ tbsp coconut oil
½ red onion, diced
1 clove garlic, finely diced
250g turkey mince
2 tsp ground cumin
1 tsp smoked paprika
salt and pepper
1 carrot, grated
1 red chilli, finely sliced – remove the seeds if you don't like it hot
½ bunch of coriander, leaves only, roughly chopped
squeeze of lemon juice
2 pitta breads, to serve

METHOD

Bring a saucepan of water to the boil, add the chickpeas and simmer for 5 minutes. Drain in a sieve or colander, then rinse under cold running water.

Meanwhile, heat the coconut oil in a large frying pan over a high heat. Add the onion and garlic and fry for 1 minute, then throw in the turkey mince and fry for 2 minutes, breaking up any big lumps as you go. Sprinkle in the cumin and paprika and fry for 30 seconds, by which time the turkey mince should be cooked. Season generously with salt and pepper, then stir in the carrot, chilli and chickpeas, using the back of your spoon to crush some of the chickpeas.

When you are happy that the turkey is fully cooked and the chickpeas are warmed through, remove the pan from the heat, stir through the chopped coriander and finish with a good squeeze of lemon juice. Load into pitta breads and eat.

PIRI PIRI RICE WITH GARLIC PRAWNS

SERVES 1

I'm a massive fan of piri piri. It's one of my favourite seasonings and tastes awesome on most things. The black-eyed beans in this recipe add an extra protein boost. This is a great dish to double up, so you'll have some for lunch or dinner the next day.

MAKE AHEAD

INGREDIENTS

1 tbsp coconut oil

2 spring onions, roughly chopped

1 red chilli, roughly chopped – remove the seeds if you don't like it hot

6 baby sweetcorn, cut in half

4 cherry tomatoes, cut in half

2 tsp piri piri seasoning

100g tinned black-eyed beans, drained and rinsed

150g pre-cooked rice

large handful of baby spinach leaves

1 large clove garlic, chopped

12 raw prawns (about 200g), peeled

squeeze of lemon juice

METHOD

Heat half of the coconut oil in a wok or large frying pan over a high heat. Add the spring onions, chilli, sweetcorn and tomato and stir-fry for about 1 minute. Add the piri piri seasoning and stir-fry for 30 seconds, then add the black-eyed beans, along with 2 tablespoons of water. Add the rice, crumbling it between your fingers as you drop it in, then stir-fry for about 2 minutes, breaking up any clumps with a wooden spoon. Add the spinach, giving it a couple of turns to help it wilt. Tip the rice and vegetables onto a plate and wipe out your frying pan.

Return the wok or pan to a high heat and add the rest of the coconut oil. When it is melted and hot, add the garlic and prawns and cook for about 1 minute, stirring every now and then, until the prawns are pink and cooked through.

Spoon the garlicky prawns over the piri piri rice, finish with a squeeze of lemon juice and eat up.

SINGAPORE NOODLES

When you finish a workout feeling ravenous, you want food, and you want it fast. This is the dish for such times. It might seem like a strange combination, but the chicken, curry powder and prawns are a total winner. If you don't fancy the combo, feel free to use either chicken or prawns – in which case, you'll need 250g chicken or 200g prawns.

MAKE AHEAD
INGREDIENTS

1 tbsp coconut oil
150g skinless chicken breast, sliced into 1cm thick strips
1 tbsp mild curry powder
8 prawns, peeled
2 spring onions, roughly chopped
1 red chilli, roughly chopped – remove the seeds if you don't like it hot
1 clove garlic, roughly chopped
50g mange tout, cut in half
6 baby sweetcorn, cut in half
200g fresh egg noodles
salt and pepper
juice of 1 lime
¼ bunch of coriander, leaves only, roughly chopped

METHOD

Heat the oil in a wok or large frying pan over a high heat. Add the chicken and fry for 1 minute, turning it a couple of times. When the chicken is no longer pink, sprinkle half of the curry powder into the wok and stir to coat the chicken strips.

Throw in the prawns and toss with the other ingredients. Add the spring onions, chilli, garlic, mange tout and sweetcorn and stir-fry for about 2 minutes or until the prawns are pink and the chicken is cooked through. Check the chicken by slicing into one of the larger pieces to make sure the meat is white all the way through, with no raw pink bits left.

Add the noodles, along with about 2 tablespoons of water – this will help to loosen any ingredients that may have stuck to the wok or pan, as well as helping to separate the noodles.

Sprinkle in the rest of the curry powder and season generously with salt and pepper. Toss everything together before piling the noodles onto a plate, drizzling over the lime juice and finishing with the chopped coriander.

#BURGERME WITH SWEET POTATO FRIES

SERVES 2

I'm sorry but I refuse to release a cookbook without at least a couple of healthy burger recipes. Burgers make me happy, and I promise this one won't disappoint. Stack it up like a boss and get it done!

INGREDIENTS

2 large sweet potatoes, cut into fries
600g reduced-fat (about 5%) beef mince
1 small red onion, finely chopped
1 clove garlic, finely chopped
salt and pepper
1 tbsp coconut oil
2 tsp chipotle paste
2 tbsp crème fraiche
2 burger buns
1 tomato, sliced
2 gherkins, sliced
lettuce, to serve

METHOD

Preheat your grill to maximum.

Zap the sweet potato fries in the microwave for 7 minutes at 900w, then leave to rest for 30 seconds.

While the sweet potato is spinning in the microwave, mix the beef with the onion and garlic – get your hands stuck in and work the ingredients together with a good pinch each of salt and pepper. Shape the mixture into two good-sized burgers about 2cm thick. Place on your grill pan or a baking tray and grill for 5 minutes on each side.

Heat the coconut oil in a large frying pan over a high heat. Add the sweet potato fries and fry for about 3 minutes on each side or until they are nicely browned all over. Drain on paper towels, then season with a good pinch of salt.

Mix together the chipotle paste and crème fraiche in a small bowl.

Cut the burger buns in half, then build your burgers: start with a beef patty, then top with tomato, gherkins, lettuce and chipotle-crème fraiche sauce, finishing with the top half of the burger bun. Serve up with the sweet potato fries and shout out 'Hashtag BurgerMe' just before you eat it.

PRAWN, COURGETTE AND LENTIL CURRY

SERVES 1

MAKE AHEAD
GOOD TO FREEZE
INGREDIENTS

½ tbsp coconut oil
1 small red onion, diced
1 courgette, diced
1 red chilli, sliced – optional
1 tbsp curry paste – I like
  Patak's rogan josh or bhuna
200g tinned chopped
  tomatoes
200g raw prawns, peeled
100g pre-cooked puy lentils
200g pre-cooked basmati rice
½ bunch of coriander, leaves
  only, roughly chopped

We usually think it takes ages to cook a curry, but some can be lightning quick to make! You can use chicken instead of prawns if you want; even a bit of haddock would be good. And if you really want to mix it up, aubergine works as well as courgette, though you'll need to cook it for a bit longer. Don't be afraid to use ready-made curry pastes, either – they are lifesavers!

METHOD

Melt the coconut oil in a wok or large frying pan over a medium to high heat. Add the onion and courgette – and the chilli, if using – and stir-fry until starting to soften.

Spoon in the curry paste and fry for 30 seconds before pouring in the chopped tomatoes. Bring to the boil, then add the prawns and lentils. Simmer the curry for 1 minute or until the lentils are warmed through and the prawns are cooked – they're done when their flesh turns vibrant pink.

Meanwhile, ping your rice in the microwave, following the packet instructions.

Stir the coriander through your curry and serve up with the rice.

MIGHTY DUCK NOODLES

It's good to switch up your bird now and again. This quick and easy duck noodle dish makes a nice change from your standard chicken and turkey. The five-spice and hoisin create an absolute explosion of flavour.

MAKE AHEAD
INGREDIENTS

½ tbsp coconut oil

1 x 240g duck breast fillet, skin removed, sliced into 1cm thick strips

½ tsp five-spice powder

3 spring onions, finely sliced

1 clove garlic, finely sliced

100g midget trees (tender-stem broccoli), any bigger stalks sliced in half lengthways

250g fresh egg noodles

2 tbsp hoisin sauce

¼ small cucumber, sliced into thin batons

METHOD

Melt the coconut oil in a wok or large frying pan over a medium to high heat. Add the duck and let it sizzle for a couple of minutes. When the duck is mostly brown, crank the heat up to high and add the five-spice powder, spring onions, garlic and midget trees, along with about 2 tablespoons of water – this will steam up and help everything to cook. Stir-fry for about 3 minutes, then add the noodles, and toss until the noodles are warmed through.

Remove from the heat and pour in the hoisin sauce. Stir everything together into one delicious mass, then slide onto a plate and top with the cucumber.

JOE'S McLEANIE BURGER

Another burger recipe? Guilty. Well, I did say I love burgers. And remember a turkey is not just for Christmas – combined with all these tasty ingredients, you really won't be disappointed with this super-lean hero burger.

SERVES 2

INGREDIENTS

400g turkey mince
3 tsp fish sauce
½ bunch of coriander, leaves only, roughly chopped
2 tsp sesame oil
4 spring onions, finely sliced
salt and pepper
2 burger buns
2 tbsp full-fat Greek yoghurt
3 tsp chipotle paste
sliced tomato and lettuce leaves, to serve

METHOD

Preheat your grill to its highest setting.

Chuck the turkey, fish sauce, coriander, sesame oil and spring onions into a large bowl. Season generously with salt and pepper, then get your hands stuck in and work the ingredients well. The more you work the meat, the better the burgers will hold together when cooked. Shape the meat into two equal patties.

Place the patties on your grill pan or a baking tray and grill the burgers for 5 minutes on each side or until they are totally cooked through. Check by slicing into one of the patties to make sure the meat is white all the way through, with no raw pink bits left.

Meanwhile, cut your burger buns in half. Mix together the yoghurt and chipotle paste and spread over the burger buns.

When your burgers are cooked, remove from the grill and build your dream burger, stacking it up with tomato and lettuce – the bigger, the better.

CHEEKY CHICKEN FRIED RICE

Do you ever just feel lazy and want to do as little work as possible in the kitchen? I do, and if you feel the same, then this one-wok, no-messing-about dish will be right up your street. Pre-cooked, packaged rice is a great thing to have in the house for a quick meal – and for this, it doesn't even have to go in the microwave. Almost any vegetables can go into this fried rice, making it a great way of using up the stragglers. It's perfect for lunch the next day too, so you can always do a cheeky double-up with the recipe. #Guilty

**SERVES
1**

MAKE AHEAD

INGREDIENTS

1 tbsp coconut oil
1 clove garlic, finely chopped
1cm ginger, finely chopped
1 x 240g skinless chicken breast fillet, sliced into 1cm thick strips
2 spring onions, roughly chopped
1 carrot, chopped into 1cm pieces
40g frozen peas
50g baby sweetcorn, roughly chopped
250g pre-cooked basmati rice
1 tbsp light soy sauce
2 tsp sesame oil
½ red chilli, finely chopped – optional

METHOD

Melt the coconut oil in a wok or large frying pan over a high heat. Throw in the garlic and ginger and stir-fry for 30 seconds.

Add the chicken and stir-fry for 2 minutes, by which time the chicken should have coloured a little on the outside. Chuck in the spring onions, carrot, peas and sweetcorn and stir-fry for another 2–3 minutes until the vegetables and chicken are cooked through. Check by slicing into one of the larger pieces of chicken to make sure the meat is white all the way through, with no raw pink bits left.

Tip in the rice straight from the packet, along with about 1 tablespoon of water, and keep stir-frying for about 1 minute or until the rice is warmed through.

Remove the wok or pan from the heat and pour in the soy sauce and sesame oil. Top with red chilli for added kick.

SERVES 2

MAKE AHEAD
GOOD TO FREEZE
(only the meatballs,
not the pasta)

INGREDIENTS

1 tbsp coconut oil
1 small red onion, diced
2 cloves garlic, finely chopped
2 sprigs of fresh thyme
1 x 400g tin of chopped
  tomatoes
12 (about 400g) ready-made
  turkey meatballs (or see
  page 93 to make your own)
2 large handfuls of baby
  spinach leaves
salt and pepper
400g fresh tagliatelle
½ bunch of basil, leaves only,
  roughly chopped

MY BIG JUICY MEATBALLS AND PASTA

Yes, that's right, pasta! Don't be scared – you can eat pasta and still burn fat. This food mountain will leave you feeling like a champion when you clear the plate. Fresh pasta cuts down the cooking time, but isn't essential. And if you can't find turkey meatballs, pork or beef meatballs work just as well.

METHOD

Start by bringing a large saucepan of water to the boil, ready to cook the pasta.

In a large frying pan or another large saucepan, heat the coconut oil over a medium to high heat. Add the onion, garlic and thyme to the pan and fry, stirring regularly, for 2 minutes or until the onion and garlic are just starting to soften. Pour in the tomatoes and bring to the boil. Carefully drop the meatballs into the sauce, then reduce the heat to a simmer and cover your pan with a lid. If you don't have a lid big enough, a large dinner plate or baking tray should do the trick. Simmer the meatballs for about 6 minutes, or until cooked through. Check by cutting into one to make sure there are no raw pink bits of meat left. Add the spinach to the sauce and stir until wilted. Season with salt and pepper, then remove the pan from the heat.

Drop the tagliatelle into the boiling water and cook for about 2 minutes. Drain the pasta and tip it back into the pan. Spoon in about half of the meatballs and sauce and mix with the pasta. Divide the saucy pasta between two plates, spoon over the remaining sauce and garnish with the basil.

SERVES
1

MAKE AHEAD
GOOD TO FREEZE

INGREDIENTS

½ tbsp coconut oil
2 spring onions, finely sliced
275g smoked haddock,
   skinned and cut into small
   chunks
1 courgette, cut into 2cm
   cubes
100g frozen peas
1 tbsp mild curry powder
1 egg
250g pre-cooked basmati rice
100ml skimmed milk
large handful of baby spinach
   leaves
1 red chilli, finely sliced –
   remove the seeds if you
   don't like it hot

KEDGEREE

This kedgeree (#weirdwordalert) tastes incredible – after a
workout, it will refuel your body and satisfy your taste buds
at the same time.

METHOD

Bring a saucepan of water to the boil, ready to poach
the egg.

Melt the coconut oil in a large frying pan over a medium
to high heat. Add the spring onions, smoked haddock and
courgette and fry for 2–3 minutes, stirring regularly. Stir in
the peas and cook until defrosted, then sprinkle in the
curry powder and cook for 1 minute.

This is a good time to carefully crack your egg into the hot
water to poach. Cook the egg for about 4 minutes for a runny
yolk, then carefully lift out with a slotted spoon and drain on
paper towels.

While the egg is poaching, add the rice to the frying pan,
crumbling it between your fingers as you drop it in, then
stir-fry for a minute or two, breaking up any clumps with
a wooden spoon. Pour in the milk and stir, then bring to
the boil and simmer for about 30 seconds. Add the spinach
and stir until wilted.

Pile the kedgeree onto a plate, top with the poached egg
and scatter with sliced chilli, then serve.

SERVES 2

MAKE AHEAD
GOOD TO FREEZE
INGREDIENTS

1 tbsp olive oil
1 red onion, diced
1 clove garlic, chopped
1 sprig of rosemary
6 sausages
1 tbsp balsamic vinegar
1 x 400g tin of chopped
  tomatoes
300g fresh gnocchi
½ bunch basil, leaves only,
  roughly chopped

GNOCCHI WITH SAUSAGE RAGU

This little Italian number is guaranteed to please. The gnocchi cooks in no time, and the sausages are already full of flavour, making this a really tasty meal for very little effort.

METHOD

Bring a large saucepan of water to the boil, ready to cook the gnocchi.

In a frying pan, heat the olive oil over a medium to high heat. Add the onion, garlic and rosemary and cook, stirring occasionally, for 2–3 minutes.

Taking one sausage at a time, squeeze tightly with your fingers about a third of the way along its length to force the meat from the sausage skin – a small ball of sausage meat should pop out of the end of the casing. Repeat the process until you have 18 balls of sausage meat. Discard the empty sausage skins.

Drop the balls of sausage meat into the frying pan, and gently tumble them around the pan to coat in the oil, onion and garlic. Crank up the heat to high and pour in the balsamic vinegar, then let it bubble away to almost nothing. Pour in the tomatoes, bring to the boil and simmer for 5–6 minutes.

Meanwhile, drop the gnocchi into the pan of boiling water and cook for about 2 minutes, or according to the packet instructions, then drain.

Check that the balls of sausage meat are fully cooked through – cut into one to make sure – then divvy up the gnocchi, top with the sausage ragu and finish with the basil.

SAMMY THE SEA BASS WITH SPAGHETTI

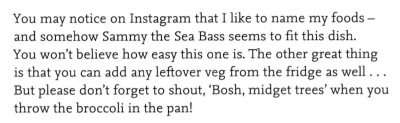

SERVES 1

You may notice on Instagram that I like to name my foods – and somehow Sammy the Sea Bass seems to fit this dish. You won't believe how easy this one is. The other great thing is that you can add any leftover veg from the fridge as well . . . But please don't forget to shout, 'Bosh, midget trees' when you throw the broccoli in the pan!

INGREDIENTS

80g dried spaghetti
½ tbsp olive oil
2 x 125g sea bass fillets,
  skin on
salt and pepper
80g midget trees (tender-
  stem broccoli), any bigger
  stalks sliced in half
  lengthways
80g kale, thick stalks removed
6 cherry tomatoes
½ red chilli, roughly sliced –
  remove the seeds if you
  don't like it hot

METHOD

Bring a large saucepan of salted water to the boil. Drop in the spaghetti and let it cook for 2 minutes less than the time given on the packet.

Meanwhile, heat the oil in a frying pan over a medium heat. Season the sea bass with salt and pepper, and when the oil is hot, gently lay the fillets in the pan, skin side down, and fry for 2–3 minutes. Flip the fish over, remove the pan from the heat and leave the fish to cook in the residual heat for 2 minutes. Carefully lift the fish out of the pan, then peel off and discard the skin.

By now the spaghetti should be almost cooked. Throw in all of the veg, and simmer with the pasta for 2 minutes. The tomatoes may split a little, but don't worry. Drain the pasta and veg in a colander.

Take the pan used to fry the fish and place it back over a medium to high heat. Tip in the spaghetti and veg, season generously with salt and pepper, and toss everything together for 1 minute – this final frying gives the dish extra flavour.

Spoon the spaghetti and vegetables into a shallow bowl, flake over the fish in large chunks and top with the sliced chilli.

CHICKEN AND QUINOA STIR-FRY

Quinoa used to be one of those obscure health foods, but these days it's everywhere – and luckily you can now get it pre-cooked in packets, so you don't have to wait 20 minutes for it to cook. The high protein content of quinoa makes this a great meal for building lean muscle.

MAKE AHEAD

INGREDIENTS

½ tbsp coconut oil
3 spring onions, finely sliced
½ red pepper, de-seeded
  and finely diced
½ courgette, diced
1 x 240g skinless chicken
  breast fillet, cut into 1cm
  thick slices
2 tsp smoked paprika
salt and pepper
225g pre-cooked quinoa
25g feta, crumbled
small bunch of parsley,
  leaves only, roughly chopped
  – optional
squeeze of lemon juice

METHOD

Melt the coconut oil in a wok or large frying pan over a medium to high heat. Add the spring onions, red pepper and courgette and stir-fry for 2–3 minutes or until the vegetables are just starting to soften.

Increase the heat to high and add the chicken, along with the paprika and a little salt and pepper. Fry for a further 3–4 minutes or until the chicken is just cooked. Check by slicing into one of the larger pieces to make sure the meat is white all the way through, with no raw pink bits left.

Stir in the quinoa and fry for a minute or so, until it is warmed through.

Serve your chicken and quinoa stir-fry topped with crumbled feta, chopped parsley (if using) and a squeeze of lemon juice.

QUICK TORTILLA PIZZA

SERVES 1

This recipe is for all the pizza lovers out there. It may not have exactly the same effect as a cheesy stuffed-crust pizza, but it's cheaper, quicker and much leaner. Feel free to change the toppings and build your own dream pizza.

INGREDIENTS

4 large handfuls of baby spinach leaves

2 large tortillas

200g tinned chopped tomatoes

200g tinned kidney beans, rinsed and drained

½ tsp dried oregano

8 black olives, pitted and cut in half

250g sliced cooked meat – I like ham or cold roast chicken

2 large eggs

salt and pepper

green salad, to serve – optional

METHOD

Put the kettle on to boil and preheat your oven to 230°C (fan 210°C, gas mark 8).

Tip the spinach into a large colander and pour over boiling water from the kettle until it wilts. Quickly run the spinach under cold water to cool, then use your hands to squeeze out as much moisture as possible.

Place the tortillas on a non-stick baking tray. Mix together the tomatoes, kidney beans and oregano, then spread over the tortillas. Divide the wilted spinach evenly between the tortillas, then scatter over the olives and meat. Make a little well in the middle of each tortilla pizza and crack in an egg. Season the pizzas with salt and pepper, then slip into the hot oven and bake for 12 minutes, or until the edges are browned and the white of the egg is set.

Slide the pizzas onto a board and serve with a big green salad . . . or just wolf down.

SPICED AUBERGINE AND CHICKPEAS WITH TURKEY

MAKE AHEAD
GOOD TO FREEZE
(the aubergine and chickpea stew, but not the turkey)

INGREDIENTS

1 tbsp coconut oil
4 spring onions, cut into 1cm slices
2 cloves garlic, finely sliced
1 small aubergine, cut into 1cm dice
1 red chilli, roughly chopped – remove the seeds if you don't like it hot
4 x 100g turkey steaks
salt and pepper
1 tsp garam masala
1 tbsp tomato puree
1 x 400g tin of chickpeas, drained and rinsed
½ bunch of coriander, leaves only, roughly chopped

Aubergine, chickpeas and Indian spices are a match made in heaven. This is a really hearty and filling post-workout meal. If you're not cooking for two, box up the rest and keep it in the fridge for tomorrow's lunch or dinner.

METHOD

Preheat your grill to its highest setting.

Heat the coconut oil in a wok or large frying pan over a medium to high heat. Add the spring onions, garlic, aubergine and chilli and stir-fry for 3–4 minutes.

While the vegetables are cooking, season the turkey steaks and grill them for 4–5 minutes on each side until cooked through. Check by cutting into the thickest part of one of the turkey steaks to make sure the meat is white all the way through, with no raw pink bits left. Remove and leave to rest.

Back to the vegetables in the wok or pan: add the garam masala and tomato puree and cook for a minute, stirring so the spices don't burn. Pour in 200ml of water, along with the chickpeas, then season generously with salt and pepper, bring to a simmer and cook for 2 minutes.

Serve up the chickpea and aubergine stew, then top with the turkey steaks and finish with the coriander.

SAUSAGE AND LENTIL CASSEROLE

SERVES 2

Don't worry, I know what you're thinking: how on earth can I make a casserole in 15 minutes? The secret to speeding this up is skinny sausages and pre-cooked lentils. It tastes just as good as any 4-hour casserole, though, so give it a crack.

MAKE AHEAD
GOOD TO FREEZE
INGREDIENTS

½ tbsp coconut oil
10 chipolata sausages
1 red pepper, de-seeded and
  thinly sliced
½ courgette, cut into
  1cm dice
10 cherry tomatoes
2 sprigs of thyme
250g pre-cooked puy lentils
150ml chicken stock
salt and pepper
½ bunch of parsley, leaves
  only, roughly chopped –
  optional

METHOD

Heat the coconut oil in a large frying pan over a medium to high heat. Add the sausages and cook for 3 minutes to brown, turning them a couple of times.

Add the red pepper, courgette, tomatoes and thyme and stir-fry for 3–4 minutes or until the vegetables are just starting to soften. Tip in the lentils, along with the stock, and season generously with salt and pepper. Mix everything together, bring to a simmer and cook for 3–4 minutes.

Make sure the lentils are hot and the sausages are cooked through, then scatter over the parsley, if using, and serve immediately.

BLACK BEAN TOFU WITH SHIITAKE AND RICE

SERVES 2

I do apologize for the lack of veggie recipes, but I'm a meat-lover myself! Here's one that vegetarians, meat eaters and pescatarians will all love, though. When cooked with the right ingredients and flavours, tofu is really tasty – and if you eat a big enough portion, you can get a decent protein hit.

MAKE AHEAD
INGREDIENTS

1 tbsp coconut oil

1 courgette, cut into 1cm dice

1 red chilli, roughly chopped –
  remove the seeds if you
  don't like it hot

2 cloves garlic, roughly
  chopped

6 spring onions, cut into 1cm
  slices

8 shiitake mushrooms,
  roughly chopped

2 tbsp black bean sauce

400g firm tofu, cut into 2cm
  cubes

250g pre-cooked jasmine or
  basmati rice

METHOD

Heat the coconut oil in a wok or large frying pan over a medium to high heat. Throw in the courgette and stir-fry for 1 minute. Add the chilli, garlic, spring onions and shiitake and stir-fry for 3–4 minutes, or until all the vegetables are starting to soften.

Spoon in the black bean sauce and pour in 150ml of water. Bring to a simmer, then drop in the tofu and simmer gently for about 2 minutes or until heated through.

Ping your rice in the microwave and divide it between two plates, then top with the spicy, rich tofu.

TERIYAKI CHICKEN STIR-FRY

SERVES 1

This is one of those dishes you'll love so much you'll want to make it every day. You can just walk in from work and smash this all in a wok, with little mess to clear up afterwards – a true Lean in 15 recipe.

MAKE AHEAD

INGREDIENTS

½ tbsp coconut oil

3 spring onions, finely sliced

2 cloves garlic, finely sliced

2cm ginger, finely chopped
  or grated

1 x 240g skinless chicken
  breast fillet, sliced into
  1 cm thick strips

2 heads of pak choy, leaves
  separated

225g fresh egg noodles

large handful of baby
  spinach leaves

½ tbsp honey

1 tbsp light soy sauce

2 tsp rice wine vinegar

1 red chilli, finely sliced –
  remove the seeds if you
  don't like it hot

METHOD

Heat the coconut oil in a wok or large frying pan over a high heat. Add the spring onions, garlic and ginger and stir-fry for 10 seconds, then add the chicken and stir-fry for 1 minute.

Throw in the pak choy, noodles, spinach and a couple of tablespoons of water – this will create steam to help cook the vegetables and separate the noodles. Stir-fry for 2–3 minutes, by which time the vegetables will have wilted and the chicken should be totally cooked through. Check by slicing into one of the larger pieces to make sure the meat is white all the way through, with no raw pink bits left.

Remove from the heat and pour in the honey, soy sauce and vinegar, mixing well. Pile the stir-fry onto a plate, top with the sliced chilli and get it down you.

★ TOP TIP

If you can't find fresh egg noodles, just use dried ones – but remember they'll need rehydrating before you add them to the stir-fry. And for a gluten-free meal, swap the soy sauce for tamari, and use rice noodles instead of egg noodles.

MAKE AHEAD

INGREDIENTS

1 x 240g skinless chicken
  breast fillet
salt and pepper
1 tbsp tomato ketchup
½ tsp smoked paprika
1 tbsp Worcestershire sauce
2 large tortilla wraps
1 baby gem lettuce, shredded
6 cherry tomatoes, halved
4 tbsp tinned black-eyed
  beans, drained and rinsed
2 tbsp cottage cheese

BIG BARBECUE CHICKEN WRAP

This easy chicken wrap with barbecue sauce goes down
a treat after a workout. Wrapped up tightly in foil, it's the
ideal lunch on the go.

METHOD

Preheat your grill to maximum.

Spread out a large piece of cling film on your chopping board
or benchtop. Lay the chicken on the cling film and place
another piece of cling film on top. Using a rolling pin, heavy
saucepan or any other blunt object, bash the chicken until
it is at least half its original thickness.

Remove the chicken from the cling film and season with
salt and pepper, then place on your grill pan or a baking tray
and grill for 4 minutes, without turning.

Meanwhile, mix together the ketchup, paprika and
Worcestershire sauce until you have a smooth barbecue sauce.
Flip the chicken over and give it 2 more minutes, then smear
over a little of the sauce and grill for a further 3–4 minutes,
or until it is fully cooked through. Check by slicing into it to
make sure the meat is white all the way through, with no raw
pink bits left.

Slice the cooked chicken into long strips. Spread the remaining
barbecue sauce over the tortillas, then top with the chicken,
lettuce, tomatoes, beans and cottage cheese. Roll up your big fat
tortillas and get munching.

TOMATO DAAL WITH CHICKEN

Clocking in at about an hour, this is another recipe that takes longer than 15 minutes. Don't be put off, though – it's full of flavour and really satisfying after a workout, so it's worth the wait. If you're after a short cut, batch-cook the daal and freeze the extra, ready for the next time.

LONGER RECIPE
MAKE AHEAD
GOOD TO FREEZE

INGREDIENTS

150g yellow split peas
1½ tbsp coconut oil
1 tsp cumin seeds
1 fresh bay leaf, or 2 dried
1 large red onion, diced
4 cloves garlic, finely chopped
2 red chillies, diced – remove the seeds if you don't like it hot
5cm ginger, diced
½ tsp ground turmeric
1 tbsp garam masala
5 large tomatoes, roughly chopped
200–250ml chicken stock
2 x 260g skinless chicken breast fillets, sliced into 1cm strips
salt and pepper
bunch of coriander, leaves only, roughly chopped

METHOD

Tip the split peas into a large bowl and cover with warm water from the tap, then leave to soak for at least 20 minutes.

Melt 1 tablespoon of the coconut oil in a large saucepan over a medium to high heat. Add the cumin seeds and bay leaf and fry for 30 seconds, then add the onion and stir-fry for 2–3 minutes or until just starting to soften and brown. Drop in the garlic, chillies and ginger and stir-fry for 1 minute.

Sprinkle in the turmeric and the garam masala and stir constantly for 30 seconds. Chuck in the tomatoes and chicken stock, then bring to the boil. Drain and rinse the soaked split peas and add them to the pan. Simmer for about 40 minutes, stirring regularly, and adding a little extra water if necessary, by which time the split peas should be completely cooked and starting to fall apart.

When the daal is nearly ready, melt the remaining coconut oil in a frying pan and add the chicken, seasoning it generously with salt and pepper. Fry for about 3 minutes or until the chicken is cooked through. Check by slicing into one of the larger pieces to make sure the meat is white all the way through, with no raw pink bits left.

Stir the coriander through the cooked daal, top with the chicken and serve.

LONGER RECIPE
MAKE AHEAD
GOOD TO FREEZE

INGREDIENTS

1½ tbsp olive oil
1kg reduced-fat (about 5%)
  beef mince
1 large red onion, diced
1 carrot, diced
1 courgette, diced
2 cloves garlic, finely chopped
1 tbsp tomato puree
400ml beef stock
1 x 400g tin of chopped
  tomatoes
18 lasagne sheets
bunch of basil, leaves only,
  roughly torn – optional
crusty bread, to serve

MY MUM'S SPECIAL LASAGNE

This is my mum's special recipe. In fact, as she would say, it's the only thing she can cook. She's Italian, and when she was growing up, she used to make this almost every week. Being a lasagne, it takes more like an hour and 15 minutes from start to finish, but it doesn't take too long to prep – and once it's in the oven you can sit back and relax. I'm sure you will love this, just like I always have.

METHOD

Heat ½ tablespoon of the olive oil in a large saucepan over a high heat. Add half the mince and fry for 2–3 minutes, stirring to break up the chunks. Tip out onto a plate, then repeat with another ½ tablespoon of oil and the rest of the mince.

When the meat has all been browned, wipe out your pan and heat the remaining ½ tablespoon of oil over a medium to high heat. Add the onion, carrot, courgette and garlic and cook, stirring regularly, for about 5 minutes – by which time the vegetables should have started to soften and colour a little. Add the tomato puree, beef stock and tomatoes, then return the mince to the pan. Bring to a simmer and cook for 20 minutes.

Preheat the oven to 190°C (fan 170°C, gas mark 5).

Start building your lasagne in a baking dish about 30cm x 15cm. Spoon in about a quarter of the meat sauce, spreading it over the base of the dish, then lay 6 sheets of pasta on top (don't worry too much if they overlap). Repeat the process until you have four layers of meat sauce and three layers of pasta – your last layer should be a layer of meat sauce. Tightly cover the dish with foil and bake in the oven for 40 minutes, or until it is heated through and the pasta is fully cooked – you should be able to easily insert a fork into the lasagne.

Finish the lasagne with a scattering of freshly torn basil, if you like, and serve with a chunk of bread and a green salad.

SPANISH OMELETTE

This super-satisfying potato omelette needs about 30 minutes of your time, but it tastes great hot or cold, and so is perfect for carrying in a lunch box to work with some fresh salad.

LONGER RECIPE
MAKE AHEAD

INGREDIENTS

12 new potatoes
1 tbsp olive oil
5 spring onions, sliced
1 red chilli, thinly sliced – remove the seeds if you don't like it hot
2 handfuls of baby spinach leaves, plus a little extra to serve
300g deli-style cooked chicken or ham, roughly torn or sliced
8 eggs
salt and pepper
bread, to serve
cherry tomatoes, to serve

METHOD

Prick the potatoes with a fork and microwave at 900w for 3 minutes. Leave them to rest for 2 minutes, then blast them for a further 2 minutes, by which time they should be cooked through. Leave to cool and then slice them up.

Preheat your grill to maximum.

Heat the olive oil in a decent non-stick frying pan (about 20cm in diameter) over a medium to high heat. Add the potatoes, and fry, turning every now and then, for 2 minutes. Add the spring onions and chilli and cook for another minute. Throw in the spinach, along with the chicken or ham, and fry for about 30 seconds or until the spinach has wilted.

Beat the eggs with a good pinch of salt and pepper, then pour into the frying pan. Use a wooden spoon or spatula to move the egg around, scraping it up from the base, for 1–2 minutes or until there is a good proportion of cooked egg in the pan. Leave the egg to cook for a minute longer, then slide the pan under the grill (if your frying pan has a plastic handle, make sure that this doesn't go under the grill!) and cook until the top of the omelette is just set.

Slide your omelette from the pan and cut it in half, then serve with a good chunk of bread and a side salad of the cherry tomatoes and the extra spinach.

LONGER RECIPE
GOOD TO FREEZE
INGREDIENTS

4 sweet potatoes, peeled and
   cut into chunks
salt and pepper
1 tbsp coconut oil
1kg reduced-fat (about 5%)
   beef mince
1 onion, roughly diced
1 red pepper, de-seeded and
   diced
2 carrots, grated
1 courgette, grated
2 tbsp tomato puree
200ml beef stock
75g frozen peas
3 tbsp Worcestershire sauce

JOE'S SWEET POTATO COTTAGE PIE

Trust me, this dish takes a little while to cook (about 1 hour and 15 minutes), but the prep is easy and once you bang it in the oven, all you need is patience! The sweet potato topping makes this a real winner.

METHOD

Preheat your oven to 200°C (fan 180°C, gas mark 6).

Bring a large saucepan of water to the boil. Add the sweet potato and simmer for about 10 minutes or until very tender. Drain in a colander, give them a little waft to get rid of some of the moisture, then tip back into the pan. Season generously with salt and pepper, then mash until reasonably smooth.

While the sweet potatoes are cooking, heat half of the coconut oil in a large frying pan or heavy-based casserole over a high heat. Add the mince and fry, breaking up any chunks, until the meat is just cooked and browned in places. Depending on the size of your pan, you may need to do this in two batches. Transfer the cooked meat to a bowl.

Heat the rest of the coconut oil in the same pan over a medium to high heat. Add the onion, red pepper, carrots and courgette and stir-fry for 5–6 minutes or until they just begin to soften. Squeeze in the tomato puree and cook, stirring, for a further 30 seconds, then tip the meat back in and stir well. Pour in the stock, bring to the boil and simmer for 20 minutes.

Remove from the heat and stir in the peas and Worcestershire sauce, then spoon into a large baking dish and top with the mashed sweet potato.

Bake your cottage pie for about 20 minutes, by which time the sweet potato topping should have crisped a little.

LONGER RECIPE
MAKE AHEAD
GOOD TO FREEZE

INGREDIENTS

1½ tbsp olive oil
1 large red onion, diced
3 cloves garlic, finely chopped
1kg turkey mince
3 large handfuls of baby
   spinach leaves
300g ricotta
salt and pepper
1 bunch of basil, leaves only,
   roughly chopped
16 dried cannelloni tubes
2 x 400g tins of chopped
   tomatoes
crusty bread and a side salad,
   to serve

SPINACH AND TURKEY CANNELLONI

This is another batch-cooking winner. Invest an hour and 15 minutes of your time, then divide your cannelloni into 4 portions and you're all set for a few days. If you don't enjoy turkey mince, just use beef mince instead.

METHOD

Preheat your oven to 180°C (fan 160°C, gas mark 4).

Heat 1 tablespoon of the olive oil in a large frying pan over a medium to high heat. Add the onion and garlic and fry for 2 minutes, stirring regularly, until the onions are soft and taking on a little colour.

Increase the heat to high, add half of the turkey mince and fry for 2–3 minutes, breaking up any lumps with your spoon as you go. Cook the mince until there is no more pink left, then tip out into a bowl. Repeat the process with the remaining olive oil and turkey mince. When this second batch of mince is browned, toss the spinach into the pan and stir until wilted, then tip the whole lot into the bowl with the rest of the mince.

Add the ricotta to the bowl, along with a generous amount of salt and pepper and half of the basil, and mix everything together well. Using your fingers and a teaspoon, stuff the cannelloni tubes with the turkey mixture – don't worry about being perfect here, any overspill can just be added into the sauce later.

When all of the tubes are full, pour one of the tins of tomatoes into the base of a large baking dish (about 30cm x 18cm) and stir through any leftover turkey mixture. Now line up the stuffed cannelloni tubes in the dish and pour over the second tin of tomatoes, then cover the dish with foil.

Bake your cannelloni for 35–40 minutes, by which time the pasta should be cooked through. Remove from the oven, scatter with the rest of the basil and serve with a side salad and chunks of bread.

SNACKS
AND
TREATS

5

TUNA TARTARE

SERVES 2

If you like sushi, you will love this tartare. Good-quality fresh tuna should be fine to eat raw, but ask at your fishmonger or the fish counter in your local supermarket to be sure, letting them know you'll be eating the fish raw. Definitely give this dish a miss if you are pregnant or have a weakened immune system.

INGREDIENTS

4 tbsp rice wine vinegar
1 tsp salt
½ cucumber, de-seeded and cut into 1cm dice
400g raw tuna, cut into 1cm dice – or smaller if you can
wholegrain rice cakes or rice crackers, to serve

METHOD

Pour the vinegar into a small bowl and thoroughly mix in the salt. Add the cucumber and leave to pickle for 5 minutes.

Drain off the vinegar and mix the lightly pickled cucumber with the tuna.

Serve up your raw fish treat with rice cakes or crackers for a delicious and different snack.

★ TOP TIP

You're working hard and training hard so why not treat yourself to one of my Lean in 15 treats? They're quite addictive, so don't get too greedy – share them with your friends! People are going to love you if you turn up to a party with healthy treats!

SWEETCORN AND FETA FRITTERS

These taste incredible and are very easy to make. They are good hot or cold, so you can make them the night before, ready to take to work in the morning. You can also double up the recipe and freeze half for another time.

MAKE AHEAD
GOOD TO FREEZE
INGREDIENTS

1 x 340g tin of sweetcorn, drained
1 red chilli, de-seeded and sliced, plus extra to serve – optional
3 spring onions, finely sliced
75g feta, crumbled
75g self-raising flour
1 egg
salt and pepper
1 tbsp coconut oil
1 avocado, sliced
juice of 1 lime, to serve
drizzle of sesame oil – optional

METHOD

Place the sweetcorn, chilli (if using), spring onion, feta, flour, egg and 50ml of water in a large bowl. Season with salt and pepper, then mix until you have a lumpy batter.

Heat half of the coconut oil in a non-stick frying pan over a low to medium heat. When the oil is hot, spoon in half of the batter, spreading it evenly around the pan. Cook the batter for about 2 minutes without flipping or budging . . . that's about time for 20 press-ups!

Flip the fritter and cook for a further 2 minutes. Remove from the pan and transfer to paper towels to drain off any excess oil while you cook the second fritter.

Serve the fritters with the avocado, a good squeeze of lime juice and, if you like, a drizzle of sesame oil and a sprinkling of chilli (see picture overleaf).

MAKE AHEAD
GOOD TO FREEZE
INGREDIENTS

1 x 160g tin of tuna, drained
1 courgette, grated
80g self-raising flour
1 egg
1 tbsp coconut oil
light soy sauce, to serve

TUNA AND COURGETTE FRITTERS

Such an awesome and tasty snack – and there's nearly always a spare tin of tuna knocking about in the cupboard. You can batch-cook and freeze these too, if you like.

METHOD

Flake the tuna out of the tin into a bowl, then add the courgette, flour and egg. Mix together to make a batter. If need be, add a dribble of water to loosen the consistency until it resembles thick double cream.

Melt a little of the oil in a frying pan over a medium heat. Spoon in large mounds of the batter, leaving some space between each one, as the batter will spread and work itself into a little puddle. Aim for fritters about 7–8cm in diameter if you want to make about a dozen – but feel free to just make four big ones instead.

Cook the fritters for about 2–3 minutes on each side before lifting them out of the pan and draining on paper towels.

Serve the fritters with a small bowl of soy sauce for dipping.

MAKES 400g

INGREDIENTS

400g cashew nuts
2 tsp olive or groundnut oil
2 tsp ground cumin
1½ tsp smoked paprika

MAKES 400g

INGREDIENTS

400g unsalted peanuts
4 tsp wasabi powder
2 tsp olive oil

MAKES 24

INGREDIENTS

3 mini tortilla wraps
a few pumps of olive oil spray
2 tsp ground cumin
1 tsp smoked paprika
1 tsp celery salt

SPICED CASHEWS

METHOD

Preheat your oven to 190°C (fan 170°C, gas mark 5).

Mix all the ingredients together, then tip onto a baking tray and roast in the oven for 12–15 minutes until the nuts are crisp and lightly coloured. Remove from the oven and sprinkle with salt. These spiced nuts will keep in an airtight container for up to 5 days.

WASABI PEANUTS

METHOD

Preheat your oven to 190°C (fan 170°C, gas mark 5).

Mix all the ingredients together, then tip onto a baking tray and roast in the oven for 12–15 minutes until the nuts are crisp and lightly coloured. Remove from the oven and sprinkle with salt. The wasabi nuts will keep in an airtight container for up to 4 days.

SPICED TORTILLA CHIPS

METHOD

Preheat your oven to 170°C (fan 150°C, gas mark 3).

Take each tortilla in turn and give it a pump of oil on both sides. Cut the tortilla into quarters, then cut each quarter in half to give you 8 triangles. Lay as many of the 24 triangles onto a baking tray as you can fit (you might have to use a couple of trays, or cook the tortilla chips in two batches).

Mix together the spices and salt until they are all well blended, then sprinkle evenly over the triangles. Bake in the oven for 6–7 minutes until lightly golden and crisp.

★ TOP TIP

Nuts are great for a party – and much healthier for you than something like crisps! But they're still a treat, so don't get too carried away. I recommend a portion of 20–30g, no more than once a day.

MIDGET TREE AND PINE NUT PESTO

This is a great snack that will keep in an airtight container in the fridge for up to 3 days. Other green veg, such as kale and spinach, work well too. I like to eat this with chopped cauliflower, carrot and cucumber for dipping.

MAKE AHEAD
INGREDIENTS

2 heads of broccoli, broken
  into florets
4 tbsp pine nuts
3 tbsp finely grated parmesan
2 bunches of basil, leaves only
1 clove garlic, roughly
  chopped
juice and finely grated zest
  of 1 lemon
75ml olive oil
salt and pepper
chopped raw vegetables,
  to serve

METHOD

Bring a saucepan of water to the boil. Drop in the broccoli florets and cook for 1 minute. Drain in a sieve or colander, then rinse under cold running water.

Tip the broccoli into a blender and add the pine nuts, parmesan, basil, garlic, lemon juice and zest and olive oil. Season generously with salt and pepper, then pulse until virtually smooth – you will most likely have to do quite a bit of pulsing and scraping.

Serve the pesto with chopped raw vegetables.

WHIPPED-UP HERBY CREAM CHEESE

This is the perfect cheese-lover's snack, and the fresh herbs used in combination are a real winner. This can be made by hand if you don't have a food processor – it just takes a bit more time.

INGREDIENTS

180g cream cheese
2 tbsp chopped chives
2 tbsp chopped tarragon
2 tbsp chopped basil
1 small clove garlic, finely
  sliced
6 sundried tomatoes, roughly
  chopped
50g walnuts, roughly
  crumbled
celery, carrot and cucumber
  sticks, to serve

METHOD

Place all the ingredients except the walnuts and the vegetable sticks in a food processor, along with about 2 tablespoons of warm water. Blitz until totally smooth.

Tip the dip into a bowl, top with the walnuts and then dig in with the celery, carrot and cucumber 'spades'.

SMOKED MACKEREL PÂTÉ

SERVES 4

Raw cauliflower florets taste amazing with this pâté, which can be kept in an airtight container in the fridge for up to 4 days.

INGREDIENTS

300g smoked mackerel
75g crème fraiche
juice of 1 lemon
freshly ground black pepper
small bunch of chives, finely
  sliced
35g walnuts, roughly
  chopped
chopped carrots, cauliflower
  florets and sliced red
  pepper, to serve

METHOD

Remove the skin from the mackerel and, using your fingers, flake the fish into small pieces. Add the crème fraiche and lemon juice, along with a good grinding of black pepper. Use a fork to mix and mash until you're happy with the consistency of your pâté – I like it with a bit of texture.

Stir in the chives, then top the pâté with the walnuts. Serve with the carrots, cauliflower and red pepper.

AVOCADO RANCH WITH DIPPING STICKS

SERVES 2

If you love avocado, this creamy ranch dip will be right up your street. It only takes about 5 minutes to make and is jam-packed with healthy fats to keep you energized.

INGREDIENTS

1 large avocado, roughly chopped

245g full-fat Greek yoghurt

juice of 1 lemon

1 clove garlic, grated or finely chopped

small handful of chives, finely chopped

small handful of dill, finely chopped

small handful of parsley, finely chopped

salt and pepper

6 large celery sticks, to serve

METHOD

Place the avocado in a food processor. Add the yoghurt, lemon juice, garlic, chives, dill and parsley. Season with salt and pepper, then process until smooth.

Serve the avocado dip with the celery sticks.

★ TOP TIP
SNACK IDEAS

If you don't have time to make a snack, here are a few ideas for you!

★ Scoop of whey protein with water

★ 20–30g nuts

★ 85g beef jerky

★ Boiled egg

★ 75–100g fruit (melon, blueberries, strawberries, raspberries, apple or pear). Please limit fruit to one snack per day and try not to have it more than a few times a week because it won't help your fat-burning.

SALMON AND AVOCADO HAND ROLL

SERVES 2

Another great snack option that's high in healthy fats. This dish is so impressive you could easily serve it as a starter at a dinner party. Just make sure you get the very freshest fish from your fishmonger – let them know you'll be serving it raw. Anyone with a compromised immune system should avoid raw fish altogether, as should pregnant women.

INGREDIENTS

400g raw salmon, cut into
  1cm dice – or smaller if
  possible
1cm ginger, finely grated
1½ tbsp light soy sauce
2 tsp sesame oil
2 tsp rice wine vinegar
1 avocado, halved and peeled
2 large sheets of nori seaweed
  (about 20cm x 20cm)
¼ cucumber, de-seeded and
  sliced into 8 batons

METHOD

Place the salmon, ginger, soy sauce, sesame oil and vinegar in a bowl and mix well.

Cut each avocado half lengthways into 4 slices, so you have 8 slices of avocado.

Cut each sheet of nori into 4 equal squares.

Spread out your nori squares and lay a slice of avocado in the middle of each one, then sit a cucumber baton alongside. Divide the salmon mixture evenly among the squares of nori, spooning it along the length of the avocado and cucumber.

Dip a finger in some water and dampen the edge of the nori squares so that they will stick.

Roll up your hand rolls and prepare to enjoy a Zen-like taste experience.

BEETROOT PROTEIN BROWNIES

MAKES ABOUT 16

I didn't want to release a cookbook without a few sweet treats. These are yummy, and way healthier than your normal chocolate brownies. But they should still be enjoyed on occasion and not scoffed every day. A slice once a week, after a workout, is fine. These take more like 30 minutes than 15 minutes to make – but hey, you have to earn your treats!

LONGER RECIPE INGREDIENTS

2 cooked and peeled beetroot (about 140g), roughly chopped
175g ground almonds
120g chestnut puree
30g cocoa powder
45g honey
1 scoop (30g) vanilla protein powder
2 tsp vanilla extract
4 eggs

METHOD

Preheat your oven to 180°C (fan 160°C, gas mark 4).

Place all the ingredients in a food processor and blitz to a smooth batter.

Tip the batter into a lined brownie tin (about 28cm x 15cm) and bake for 18 minutes.

Remove the brownie from the oven and leave to cool slightly before cutting into squares and chomping down.

POST-WORKOUT POWER SQUARES

LONGER RECIPE
MAKE AHEAD

INGREDIENTS

12 pitted dates
100g rice cakes
220g rolled oats
1 scoop (30g) vanilla protein powder
2 apples, cored and grated
½ tsp baking powder
100g dried cherries, halved

Here's another tasty treat that can be whipped up inside half an hour. But don't forget these aren't for everyday eating. Enjoy them no more than once a week and share them with friends, so you don't scoff all 24 on your own! There's no excuse for 'eating them up' so they won't go to waste either, as they'll last for 5 days in an airtight container.

METHOD

Preheat your oven to 160°C (fan 140°C, gas mark 3).

Bring the kettle to the boil. Cover the dates with boiling water and leave to soak for 5 minutes.

Blitz the rice cakes in a food processor until they are totally broken down into fine crumbs. Tip them out into a large bowl.

Drain the dates, blitz in the food processor until smooth and add to the bowl with the rice cakes, along with the remaining ingredients. Mix everything together until thoroughly combined – the mixture can be a bit stiff, so get your hands in there if need be.

Tip the mixture into a lined brownie tin (about 28cm x 15cm) and bake for 25 minutes. Leave to cool before cutting into squares.

LONGER RECIPE
MAKE AHEAD
INGREDIENTS

175g mixed nuts – I like
  cashews, pecans, walnuts,
  almonds
1 tsp ground cinnamon
1 apple, cored and grated,
  skin and all
150g rolled oats
20g honey
40g raisins

JOE'S GRANOLA

Why buy sugary processed granolas when, with half an hour to spare, you can make your own healthy version at home? This goes really well with Greek yoghurt and some fresh berries at breakfast time. Don't rely on it every day, though. Nothing beats eggs for breakfast.

METHOD

Preheat your oven to 180°C (fan 160°C, gas mark 4).

Mix all the ingredients except the raisins in a large bowl, then tip onto a large baking tray, spreading it out into a single layer.

Bake for 25 minutes, pulling out the tray a couple of times and mixing everything around so the granola toasts evenly.

Remove from the oven and leave to cool before stirring in the raisins. The granola will keep in a well-sealed jar for at least 2 days – although I bet it doesn't last that long!

JOE'S PROTEIN RICE PUDDING

If you have a sweet tooth, then this is a nice snack to enjoy after a workout, particularly with some fresh berries. Allow about half an hour to make this one.

LONGER RECIPE INGREDIENTS

100g pudding rice
500ml almond milk
1 tbsp honey
1 scoop (30g) vanilla protein powder

METHOD

Place the rice, almond milk, honey and 150ml of water in a saucepan. Bring to the boil and simmer for 20–25 minutes, stirring regularly, especially towards the end, when it will become creamy and thick.

Remove from the heat and leave to cool a little before stirring through the protein powder. Do not add the protein powder with the pan on the heat, or the whey will cook and go lumpy.

Eat the pudding straight away. Or, for a more indulgent finish, pour into a baking dish and place under a hot grill until the top is nicely browned and lightly crisp.

BANANA AND PECAN CUPCAKES

MAKES 12

INGREDIENTS

100g pecans, plus 12 extra
   for decorating
70g chestnut puree
3 very ripe bananas, peeled
   and roughly sliced (you need
   about 190g flesh)
30g honey
1 scoop (30g) vanilla protein
   powder
2 tsp vanilla extract
50g ground almonds
4 eggs
12 tsp crème fraiche

Ready in 20 minutes, these are my favourite treat and quite addictive, so again go easy on them. You won't burn fat eating them every day, so save them for a special treat or make them for a party with friends. The blacker the banana, the better – seriously, totally black is fine for these.

METHOD

Preheat the oven to 190°C (fan 170°C, gas mark 5) and line a 12-hole cupcake tin with paper cases.

Place all the ingredients except the extra pecans and the crème fraiche in a food processor and blend until you have a smooth, runny batter.

Divide the batter evenly between the cupcake cases and bake for 18 minutes, or until risen and lightly golden on top.

Leave to cool, then decorate each cupcake with a teaspoon of crème fraiche and a pecan.

CHEAT'S BANANA AND ALMOND ICE CREAM

LONGER RECIPE
(quick to make, but needs
4 hours in the freezer)
MAKE AHEAD
INGREDIENTS

4 bananas, peeled and cut
   into roughly similar-sized
   chunks
1 tbsp almond butter
50ml almond milk
1 scoop (30g) vanilla protein
   powder
toasted flaked almonds, to
   serve – optional

I love ice cream, so I thought I would share this healthier cheat's ice cream recipe with you. Feel free to add other frozen fruit, such as strawberries or raspberries, to mix up the flavour.

METHOD

Line a baking tray with greaseproof paper and spread the banana chunks over it in a single layer. Place the tray in your freezer and freeze for a minimum of 4 hours, or until the banana chunks are frozen solid.

Tip the frozen banana into a food processor, along with the almond butter, almond milk and the protein powder, then pulse until virtually smooth.

Serve your cheat's ice cream topped with the toasted almonds, if using.

CHOCOLATE AND ALMOND PROTEIN CAKE

SERVES 6

LONGER RECIPE
MAKE AHEAD

INGREDIENTS

120g pitted dates
125g chestnut puree
10g cocoa powder, plus a little extra for dusting
100g ground almonds
100g chocolate (85% cocoa), melted
2 scoops (60g) vanilla protein powder
4 eggs
juice and finely grated zest of 1 orange

Well, I can't pretend this is particularly healthy, but everyone needs a treat sometimes – and, as treats go, this one is packed with nutritional goodness! The higher the percentage of cocoa in chocolate, the better it is for you – I've gone for 85% here. And if you don't have chestnut puree, feel free to substitute almond butter. You'll need to allow 30 minutes to make this cake.

METHOD

Preheat your oven to 180°C (fan 160°C, gas mark 4) and line a 23cm round cake tin with baking parchment.

Bring the kettle to the boil. Pour 150ml of boiling water over the dates and leave to soak for 5 minutes.

Tip the soaked dates, along with their soaking water, into a food processor and puree until smooth. Then add the remaining ingredients and blitz into a smooth batter.

Pour the batter into the prepared tin and bake for 20 minutes. The cake will rise in the oven, but collapse again as it cools.

Remove the cake from the tin, dust with the extra cocoa powder . . . and head to the gym for a workout, so you can properly enjoy your treat afterwards!

6

BURN FAT AND BUILD LEAN MUSCLE WITH HIIT

HIGH INTENSITY INTERVAL TRAINING (HIIT)

HIIT is one of the most effective training methods for burning fat. It might sound a bit scary, but it's not, as it's all relative to your own fitness and abilities. Everyone on my 90 Day Shift, Shape and Sustain plan, regardless of age or fitness levels, does it – with incredible results. Not only does it burn fat fast, but it also gets you outrageously fit by massively improving your cardio-vascular fitness. Every session should be hard work, but the good news is it's all over in less than 20 minutes and you will feel like an absolute winner after each session. And when your body fat melts away, it's all worth it.

WHAT IS IT?

HIIT involves short bursts of maximal effort, followed by recovery periods of low-intensity activity or rest, i.e. 20 seconds of work, followed by 40 seconds of rest. You repeat this for 15–20 minutes and that's it. Job done. Bye bye, body fat!

As I said, it's all relative to your fitness levels, so let's take a treadmill, for example: if you're a beginner, HIIT could mean an incline power walk or a jog; if you're much fitter, then it could mean a sprint. The aim is to elevate your heart rate to near maximum during the intense working sets, before letting it recover in the rest periods.

Unlike low-intensity cardio, such as steady jogging, which only burns calories during the actual workout, HIIT burns calories for up to 18 hours afterwards. This is known as the after-burn effect, where your body is working hard to repay the oxygen debt in your system and restore itself to a resting state. During this time your metabolic rate is elevated, so your body burns more calories and therefore more fat. The more intense your workout, the greater your oxygen debt will be, so you should always aim to push yourself as hard as possible. Check with your doctor first if you have any health issues. If you can talk, text or tweet during a HIIT session, then you aren't working hard enough – so get in the zone, focus and train like a super-hero!

HOW DO I DO IT?

HIIT principles can be applied to any cardio machine, such as a treadmill, cross-trainer, rowing machine or exercise bike, or to

> **Get in the zone, focus and train like a super-hero!**

body-weight exercises like burpees, mountain climbers, skipping or sprints.

Choose an exercise or combination of exercises that are suitable for you and which challenge you. You could do the same type of HIIT each time or you can change it up, i.e. rowing machine one day and then cross-trainer the next. As long as you are working hard and enjoying your training, it's all good.

WARM UP

Always carry out an exercise-specific warm up before starting your HIIT. For example, if you are going to do treadmill sprints, I recommend a power walk or slow jog before you start to sprint. The aim of a warm up is to prime your muscles and joints for the exercise they're about to perform. This is really important to prevent injuries and ensure you get the most out of your workouts, so don't be naughty and skip your warm up!

WORKOUT

Once you've warmed up, you can start your HIIT. I find the most effective protocol is a work:rest ratio of 1:2, meaning you rest for twice as long as you work. This allows you to really smash your working set and get a good recovery.

FOR EXAMPLE

> Working set of 20 seconds
> with a resting set of 40 seconds

OR

> Working set of 30 seconds
> with a resting set of 45 or 60 seconds

The effort must come in the working sets, so choose the timings that best suit you. During the resting sets, you can either slow down or come to a complete stop. You will repeat this for 15–20 minutes. It may not seem like much – but trust me, this is enough to create a calorie deficit. And if you fuel your body with the right macronutrients, you will start to see your body transform. Remember that over-training is NOT necessary, so don't get all carried away by doing two HIIT sessions per day. This will actually be counterproductive for your fat loss. Do one session, do it properly, and you won't want to do it again!

'DO ONE SESSION, DO IT PROPERLY, AND YOU WON'T WANT TO DO IT AGAIN!'

Here are two workouts for you to try out at home. My advice would be to do both workouts twice each week (so four in total), then add in an extra HIIT, if you fancy it.

WORKOUT 1: *CARDIO HIIT*

//

This workout involves three body-weight exercises that are guaranteed to get your heart rate up and your body fat melting. You need no equipment and only a small space, so you could do this in the garden or living room.

1. **High knees**

2. **Mountain climbers**

3. **Burpees**

»

1. **20 seconds High knees 40 seconds rest**

2. 20 seconds Mountain climbers
40 seconds rest

3. 20 seconds Burpees
40 seconds rest

Repeat this circuit 5 times, making a total of 15 minutes. If you find this too easy, work for 30 seconds and rest for 30 seconds.

Cool down

Cooling down is really important for your muscles and joints. Have a slow walk or cycle to let your heart rate return to normal. Static stretching or foam rolling can really help reduce your muscle soreness. You may find you experience DOMS (Delayed Onset Muscle Soreness) after your first few sessions. This is totally normal and lasts between 24 and 72 hours. Don't worry, it will pass. It's just your body's way of letting you know you've worked hard, and it will reward you by growing stronger and leaner.

When do I do it?

HIIT cardio is effective at any time of day, so I always recommend doing it when you have the most energy. This could be in the morning before work or late in the evening. Remember, this is your time to 'earn' your post-workout carbs.

How often do I do it?

You should aim to do HIIT 4 or 5 days a week for maximum results. If you can't manage that many workouts each week, that's fine – just do what you can and keep a good routine. Remember, though, that on rest days you will be consuming 3 meals from the reduced-carbohydrate menu, so if you want to enjoy your carbs, then you are going to need to find time to smash out a quick HIIT.

Good luck with your workouts. Remember to push yourself and aim to progress each week: this could mean going 0.5km/h faster each week on the treadmill or increasing the weight of your dumbbells by 1kg each week. With progression comes strength, and a strong lean body is exactly what you will earn. Be patient and be consistent. Rome wasn't built in a day.

> ❛ Be patient and be consistent ❜

WORKOUT 2: *RESISTANCE HIIT*

////////////////////////////////

This full-body workout is going to take a bit longer than the HIIT cardio one, as it's going to focus not only on elevating your heart rate, but also on increasing lean muscle with resistance training. By increasing your lean muscle mass, you will increase your metabolic rate, which means you will burn even more fat and can enjoy more food as you get leaner.

All you will need for this is a set of dumbbells for added resistance and an exercise mat. If you are a beginner, start with light weights and aim to increase them as you get stronger. You are going to do the following exercises in a circuit and perform as many reps as possible in 30 seconds. You will then rest for 45 seconds between each exercise. As you get fitter and stronger, you can reduce the rest time to 30 seconds or increase the total number of rounds of 5 full circuits.

1. **Press-ups with dumbbell row**
2. **Dumbbell squats**
3. **Shoulder presses**
4. **Dumbbell lunges**
5. **Bicep curls**

1. **30 seconds Press-ups with dumbbell row**
(You can do these on your knees if you prefer.)
45 seconds rest

2. 30 seconds
Dumbbell squats
45 seconds rest

3. 30 seconds Shoulder presses
45 seconds rest

4. 30 seconds Dumbbell lunges
45 seconds rest

5. **30 seconds**

   Bicep curls

   45 seconds rest

Repeat this circuit 3–5
times depending on
your fitness level
(approximately 30
minutes).

RESULTS: MY LEAN WINNERS

7

MY LEAN WINNERS

//

For me, one of the most rewarding things about the 90 Day Shift, Shape and Sustain plan is seeing the incredible transformations of my clients, and reading their testimonials. I call them my lean winners – and, although I never actually get to meet them, I'm proud of them all. Not everyone wants to share their stories online and most of those who do want to remain anonymous, but their progress pictures really inspire people. The daily transformations I post on Instagram are one of the reasons so many people have signed up to the plan.

There's nothing better than seeing people of all ages, shapes and sizes succeed in their goals. Often many of them have battled with their weight for years on diets, but in 90 days they transform their body and their relationship with food forever. Knowing that I have educated someone and improved their health and self-confidence is what inspires me to work even harder to help more people. My plan isn't all about weight loss. I have helped people with IBS (irritable bowel syndrome), diabetes, underactive thyroid glands, PCOS (polycystic ovary syndrome) and many other conditions to improve their way of life.

I could fill a whole book with transformations and my graduate heroes, but unfortunately I can only include a handful here. To see more lean winners, visit thebodycoach.co.uk and check out the Transformations gallery, where you'll find thousands of inspirational people, all winning their own little battles and getting fitter and stronger.

Here are just a few of the transformations from the plan (for privacy reasons, I have not included faces or @names), showing some 4-week, 8-week and 12-week transformations, to give you a better idea of the results achieved.

★

'The 90 Day SSS plan has changed my life. The education I have received has been invaluable, and I can't recommend this plan enough! I finally feel in control of my diet and my training. I LOVE the gym, and I love the feeling of being full and satisfied from nutritious healthy food. I feel immensely proud, and will be celebrating with a treat tonight before getting right back on that wagon and back in the gym in the morning!!! This is me now: fit, healthy and happy.' Sarah

★

'The amount of food was unbelievable. It took a while to get used to it, but once I got the hang of it, it was so simple. My body shape is still changing for the better, and I'm so happy with it. I am so much stronger and feel great!' Jason

90 DAY**SSS**   90 DAY SSS GRADUATE

★

'I cannot believe the #90daysssplan is already over – it's absolutely flown by. To say I'm extremely pleased with the progress is an understatement! Towards the end of last year I hit a real low. I hated my body and the way I looked, and finally decided to pluck up the courage and do something about it. Life did throw me a few curve balls during cycle 3, so I haven't been able to follow the plan 100%, but I always tried to make up for it the following day with an extra-hard HIIT session. I've done all my workouts from home, so there really are no excuses! Thank you for giving me the confidence I never had.' **Kerry**

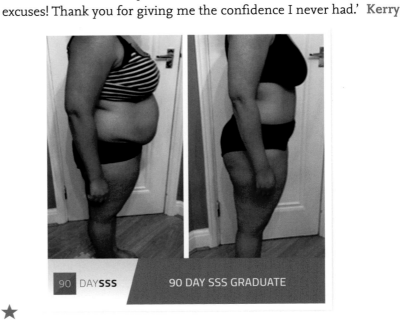

90 DAY**SSS**   90 DAY SSS GRADUATE

★

'I'm so happy that I decided to contact Joe. He has honestly changed my life. I really had zero confidence after having children, but since being on the plan not only has my confidence increased ten-fold, it has pushed me to do things in my life that I would have previously been scared to do. Because I'm feeling better, the relationships around me are more positive, and I can play with my children without getting tired. I feel motivated to carry on. The help from Joe has been invaluable and also the kind words from others doing the plan on social media. What he's telling others about healthy fats and body image is so incredibly important, regardless of whether you want to lose weight, gain weight or just get healthy – Joe's plan is a way of life, and the energy and passion behind it make you want to listen. I've even put my scales away. Thank you so much, Joe!' Jihan

90 DAY**SSS**   CYCLE ONE – 4 WEEK RESULTS

★

'I signed up to the #90daysssplan after seeing the amazing results one of my friends had. I have done every diet you can imagine, but have never seen results like those I got with The Body Coach. I really, really love food and love big portions, so every diet I have ever tried, I have struggled with hunger and cravings, but not on this one. I couldn't quite get my head around how I could eat this much and still lose weight, as I have always thought the less you eat the more you lose. The workouts are tough, but they are only about 25 minutes long, so easy enough to get through. In cycle one I tended to do them at home, following YouTube videos or using an interval timer app – which literally meant that after 25 minutes I was all done and could enjoy my yummy meal.' Sophie

90 DAY**SSS**   CYCLE TWO – 8 WEEK RESULTS

★

'The workouts are brilliant – I loved mixing HIIT and using weights, and I could feel myself getting stronger each week. Although I haven't stuck to the food side of things as well as I could have, due to being on Easter holidays, having a few boozy nights out and going away for 5 days, I can honestly say I haven't missed a workout!' Sarah

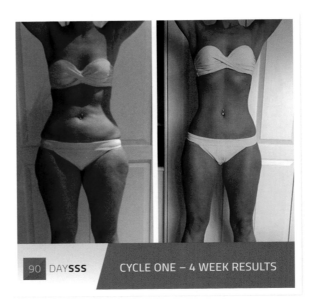

90 DAY**SSS**   CYCLE ONE – 4 WEEK RESULTS

★

'I started following Joe on Instagram and signed up straight away when I saw all the amazing transformation photos. For years I have tried every single low calorie diet and have always been unhappy with my body, especially my tree trunk legs, and was obsessed with the sad step! After seeing my own transformation photo I was shocked that the "tree trunks" had finally started to shrink. I never thought they would as I always assumed I was just a big-legged girl and no matter what exercise I did or what low-calorie diet I was on, my legs would just stay the same! Considering I used to be obsessed with weighing myself daily, after seeing my photo I think it's amazing that I actually weigh exactly the same as when I started but have lost a whole 10 inches from my body. I definitely will never be obsessed again with what the sad step has to say! I did have a few cheat days, but I stuck to the HIIT sessions 100% which I really enjoyed and can't wait to introduce the weights in cycle 2!' **Rhonda**

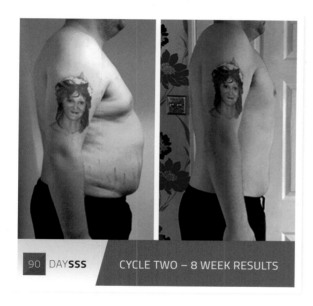

90 DAY**SSS**   CYCLE TWO – 8 WEEK RESULTS

★

'For months, even years, I never gave a thought to the food I would eat – and this, combined with no exercise at all and obviously getting older, took a massive toll on my body. Around Christmas last year I looked in the mirror and just realized I really needed to do something. I found Joe purely through chance, with a friend liking one of his videos. I then investigated further and liked the way Joe incorporated humour into fitness and nutrition. This, coupled with the results, made me take the plunge and sign up to the #90dayssplan. Having a complete lack of fitness, I found the first weeks of HIIT tough – I knew I would – but my own determination to plough on, and the support from The Body Coach team, pushed me through. Soon after, I was finding I was enjoying sweating like an absolute beast at 6am . . . strange, I know! Incorporating the weights into cycle two for me was totally alien, having never used weights before! Preparation is most definitely key. I spend around 2 hours in the kitchen on a Sunday, and this sets me up for the week.' **Danny**

MY TYPICAL WEEK

/////////////////////////////////////

I thought it would be useful to show you how I eat in a typical week, to give you ideas for your own meal planning. You'll notice I eat some of the same meals more than once a week, as I like to batch-cook and keep meals in the fridge for when I'm busy. This really helps me stay on track, as I'm far less likely to grab junk food on the go when I know I have my meals waiting at home when I get in.

You'll also notice that I always have a protein shake with honey immediately after I train. The glucose elevates my blood sugar levels post-workout, triggering the release of insulin, which will send protein to my muscles and start repairing them. When I have a protein shake as a snack at any other time of the day, I don't add honey, but just mix a scoop of protein with some ice and water.

I usually eat my post-workout meal about an hour after I finish a workout, but you can eat sooner or later if you prefer. No matter how early or late you train, you must always choose a carbohydrate-refuel meal after your workout. This is the time your muscles really need to be topped up with glycogen and fed protein to build and repair muscle tissue.

You may think I'm a bit odd eating burgers or stir-fries for breakfast, but I'm giving my body exactly what it needs to burn fat and build lean muscle. Once you start to think outside the cereal box and get over the idea of eating what feels like dinner at breakfast, you'll soon get used to it. Your work colleagues may think you're mad pulling out a chicken stir-fry at 9am, but while they're eating their sugary cereal and gaining body fat, you'll be winning and burning body fat.

The most important thing is to make your meal plan suit your lifestyle, so be flexible in your approach. As long as you consume your 3 meals and 2 snacks at some point during the day, you will burn fat and build lean muscle.

JOE'S PROTEIN SHAKE

1 scoop (30g) vanilla protein powder
15g honey
100g baby spinach leaves
handful of ice cubes

METHOD

Throw everything in the blender with a good splash of water and blitz until smooth.

/////////////////////////

	MONDAY	TUESDAY	WEDNESDAY	THURSDAY	FRIDAY	SATURDAY	SUNDAY
Training: am	7am Cardio HIIT		7am Resistance HIIT		7am Resistance HIIT	Rest day	Rest day
Post workout	Joe's protein shake		Joe's protein shake		Joe's protein shake		
Meal 1	Build-up bagel	Poached salmon with bacon	Protein pancakes	Griddled midget trees and spears with eggs	Bad-boy burrito	Griddled midget trees and spears with eggs	Cinnamon reduced-carb oatmeal
Snack	30g nuts	Apple	Avocado ranch dip	75g blueberries	Whipped-up herby cream cheese with celery	30g nuts	Protein shake
Meal 2	Lamb koftas with Greek salad	Turkey meatballs with feta	Goan fish curry	Asian duck salad	Turkey mince lettuce boats	Joe's chicken pie	Thai green chicken curry
Snack	Protein shake	Tuna and courgette fritters	30g nuts	Protein shake	30g nuts	Whipped-up herby cream cheese with celery	Protein cupcakes
Training pm		6pm Cardio HIIT		6pm Cardio HIIT		Rest day	Rest day
Post workout		Joe's protein shake		Joe's protein shake			
Meal 3	Teriyaki salmon with courgette noodles	Thai beef stir-fry	Sea bass with spiced cauliflower, peas and paneer	In-a-hurry curry fried rice	Joe's chicken pie	Eat out*	Lamb koftas with Greek salad

*Keeping it lean when eating out

· · · · · · · · · · · · · · · · · · ·

One of my favourite things in the world is eating out with family and friends. I have a very simple philosophy when it comes to 'cheat' meals. If I know I am going to go for a blow-out meal, then I like to earn it beforehand with a quick 20-minute HIIT session, so I can enjoy the extra carbs and treats as my refuel meal. If I go out for a meal when I haven't trained, then I try to stick to just fats and proteins and leave the carbs alone, opting for something like grilled steak or fish with lots of vegetables and a big drizzle of olive oil. These small food choices really will make a big difference over time and allow you to stay lean.

	MONDAY	TUESDAY	WEDNESDAY	THURSDAY	FRIDAY	SATURDAY	SUNDAY
Training: am							
Post workout							
Meal 1							
Snack							
Meal 2							
Snack							
Training pm							
Post workout							
Meal 3							

USE THIS TABLE TO PLAN YOUR OWN MEALS AND WORKOUTS FOR THE WEEK

Prepping like a boss

. . . .

I hope you love the food in this book as much as I do, and get inspired to start cooking more and prepping like a boss so you can achieve the healthy body you want. Just remember that fat loss takes time, dedication and consistency. You can and will get lean – just keep working hard and make it a habit to eat the Lean in 15 way.

LEAN IN 15 HEROES

90 DAY SSS GRADUATE

90 DAY SSS GRADUATE

CYCLE ONE – 4 WEEK RESULTS

CYCLE TWO – 8 WEEK RESULTS

CYCLE ONE – 4 WEEK RESULTS

CYCLE TWO – 8 WEEK RESULTS

CYCLE ONE – 4 WEEK RESULTS

CYCLE ONE – 4 WEEK RESULTS

CYCLE TWO – 8 WEEK RESULTS

90 DAY SSS GRADUATE

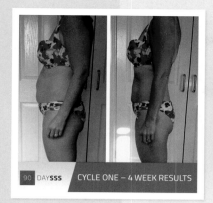

90 DAY**SSS** CYCLE ONE – 4 WEEK RESULTS

90 DAY**SSS** CYCLE TWO – 8 WEEK RESULTS

90 DAY**SSS** CYCLE ONE – 4 WEEK RESULTS

90 DAY**SSS** CYCLE TWO – 8 WEEK RESULTS

90 DAY**SSS** CYCLE TWO – 8 WEEK RESULTS

90 DAY**SSS** CYCLE TWO – 8 WEEK RESULTS

90 DAY**SSS** 90 DAY SSS GRADUATE

90 DAY**SSS** 90 DAY SSS GRADUATE

90 DAY**SSS** CYCLE TWO – 8 WEEK RESULTS

90 DAY**SSS** 90 DAY SSS GRADUATE

90 DAY**SSS** CYCLE ONE – 4 WEEK RESULTS

90 DAY**SSS** CYCLE ONE – 4 WEEK RESULTS

INDEX

ACKNOWLEDGEMENTS

I would like to start by thanking everyone who has ever completed my 90 Day plan and followed me on social media. Because of you, I've been able to build a following, spread my message and have the opportunity to release this book. Without you, I would just have been a dude in a kitchen talking to midget trees, so thanks for sticking around and sharing my videos with others.

I would also like to say thank you to all my friends and family who love and support me in my goals.

See you in June for *Lean in 15*, volume 2 – *The Shape Plan*.

CREDITS

Publisher: Carole Tonkinson
Assistant Editor: Olivia Morris
Design: Ami Smithson
Desk Editor: Claire Gatzen
Food Photography: Maja Smend
Fitness Photography: Glen Burrows
Food Styling: Bianca Nice
Prop Styling: Lydia Brun
Make-up Artist: Jo McKenna

COMING SOON

LEAN IN 15 AROUND THE WORLD

Tag your own pictures from around the world with the hashtag #Leanin15

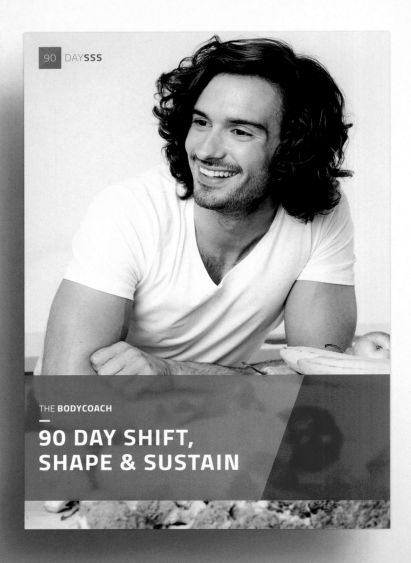

90 DAY**SSS**

To get your tailored plan and
start your transformation visit
www.thebodycoach.co.uk

Joe's 30-Minute Meals

30-Minute Meals

100 QUICK AND HEALTHY RECIPES

JOE WICKS
The Body Coach

bluebird
books for life

CONTENTS

Joe's 30-Minute Meals

Thanks so much for deciding to pick up this book. I'm really excited to be sharing my favourite 30-minute recipes with you. My aim with this – as with all of my books – is to inspire you to cook simple, quick and healthy recipes that will help you to feel great.

Ever since I learned to cook healthy food and realized what a massive difference fuelling myself with fresh, home-cooked food made to my energy levels and mood, I've wanted to get as many people as possible cooking.

Nothing makes me happier than meeting people who have never really enjoyed cooking before or have no confidence in the kitchen but are now enjoying cooking using my recipes. I met a husband who said he hadn't cooked once for his wife until he picked up my book and now cooks a recipe every night of the week for her. I believe there's no greater feeling than getting confident in the kitchen and learning how to make healthy, tasty food at home for yourself, partner or kids.

When I started creating recipe books, I focused on speed. Who doesn't want a 15-minute meal they can whip up straight after work when they are absolutely starving? I wanted to stop people just going for the easy option – the greasy takeaway or kebab – and realize they could make something that tastes way better in the same amount of time.

Sometimes, 15 minutes just isn't enough time as it means the cooking methods are a bit limiting. With this book, I'm still about speed and keeping prep time down to a minimum. After all, half an hour isn't much – especially if we've planned ahead and prepped like a boss. And I don't know about you, but once I start getting stuck in to the kitchen, I find it really fun.

To sustain long-term success, it's really important to keep your diet varied and your flavours interesting. That's what *Joe's 30-Minute Meals* sets out to do. Some of the recipes you just assemble super quickly and bung in the oven, then you can chill out with your partner or family or even better sneak in a cheeky workout. Some of the recipes like Dukkah-spiced Chicken (see page 93) are a little more work, but totally worth it on the flavour front.

ANYBODY CAN DO IT

When I started to try to create healthy meals, I didn't even know how to cook an egg properly or which flavours go well together.

But once I got going, there was no stopping me. It's amazing how much you can learn when it comes to cooking techniques and understanding flavours. This book is going to give you the confidence you need to whip up delicious food so you never have to go back to the ready meals and takeaways that don't do anything for your long-term health or happiness.

And you don't need to be a trained cook. My recipes are simple and straightforward with some shortcuts. It's all about putting good flavours together – and that's not hard.

Some people tell me they think they can't do this because they have never cooked or they don't come from a family where everyone sat around the table over delicious home-cooked food. I didn't. And if I can learn to cook – and even write six cookbooks – anybody can do it. It's just about doing a little planning and making a start and the recipes in this book will be the perfect starting point.

CHAPTERS IN THIS BOOK

I've organized this book by main ingredients: All-Day Breakfast, Chicken, Beef and Pork and so on. I hope this makes it easy for you to find the recipes you want really fast. I genuinely think there is something for everyone in this book with a real variety ranging

from easy Asian stir-fries and curries to tasty Italian pastas and risottos. Be sure to give my Sausage & Mushroom Pie a go if you loved the pies in my previous books (see page 177).

I've also added some sweet treats because everyone deserves a treat now and again. And some of these treats are still pretty healthy like my Baked Maple Apples and Blackcurrant Poached Pears (see pages 219 and 220).

PART OF A HEALTHY LIFESTYLE

Although there's no exercise in this book, any of you who know me will know that for me, good food is just one part of living a healthy lifestyle. The other big factor is being active.

My philosophy around food and fitness is really the same thing: it's all in your hands. You can create the kind of life you want – even if it feels daunting and you have never done any exercise before or cooked anything from scratch. It's never too late to start living the life you really want to live – and when that looks like eating Teriyaki Ginger Chicken (yes please) or Swedish-style Meatballs, you'll find yourself so motivated you won't even believe it. None of this is complicated.

In this book you'll find recipes that are perfect for a lazier day when you're not getting up to much activity (hopefully just a couple of days a week!). I've labelled those reduced-carb. Other recipes are to replenish your energy when you've done a workout. Those are labelled carb-refuel dishes. It's important to keep it balanced and varied.

My advice is to do four or five quick workouts a week. And when I say quick, I really mean it. They often come in at under 20 minutes. I'm a fan of High Intensity Interval Training (HIIT for short) and you can find hundreds of my free workouts on my Youtube channel – TheBodycoachTV. You can do them in your front room or the park – you don't even need any equipment. And the more energy you burn, the more you can tuck in to my carb-rich favourites like Chicken Fried Rice (see page 44) and my Tandoori Cod Burgers (see page 110).

ENJOYING LIFE

Feeling energized and fuelling your body with healthy nutrient-rich food is important. But I don't want you to feel like this is just another thing you 'have' to do – like a New Year Resolution or a 30-day programme. I do this because it makes me feel great. And I really believe you're going to feel great and have more energy and fun if you treat yourself to the delicious food in this book.

Today there's more talk about mental health than ever before. The way I look at it, we have to begin at the basics. What are we eating? Are we moving enough? Exercise is one of the biggest stress-busters around. And we all know the low mood that can come from overdoing it on the sugar front or eating junk food and relying on caffeine for energy. The recipes in this book are going to fuel your body and give you energy all day long.

I'm passionate about making sure I can do my part to help people find easy ways to work healthy habits into their lives. And I love to do that with my workouts, with a free schools HIIT programme and of course most of all with my recipes. What I'm about is fun and feeling good. And I know from my own life – and the tens of thousands of people I've now worked with – that eating generous portions of incredible food and maintaining a healthy exercise regime (without overdoing the hours in the gym so there's no time for living) is the secret to a happier life.

I hope you enjoy my new recipes and the energy they give you.

LOVE,

Joe Wicks

STAY IN TOUCH

@thebodycoach

The Body Coach TV

Stocking up

I'm always banging on about the importance of meal preparation – I call it 'prepping like a boss'! And one thing that really makes it easy to cook healthy and tasty food, is stocking up on key ingredients so you have them to hand when you need them. Then you can just pick up some chicken or sea bass or something on the way home from work and you're good to go.

I've put my favourite standby ingredients down here. Most of them are ordinary things you'll use again and again. A few are a bit more like treats, and they can seem pricey, but when you add up what you're likely to save on take-aways, ready meals and frozen pizza, you'll see that you're winning on cost as well as creating much healthier, better-tasting grub.

FRESH & FROZEN

Basics

- Tortilla wraps
- Garlic
- Ginger
- Onions (such as white, red, spring, shallots)
- Eggs
- Greek yoghurt

- Basic cheese (such as mature cheddar, goat's cheese, parmesan, mozzarella, feta)
- Avocado
- Fresh greens (such as kale, spinach, pak choy, watercress, brussels sprouts, cabbage)

- Midget trees
- Salad greens (such as lettuce, rocket, cucumber, radishes)
- Mushrooms
- Sweet potatoes
- Aubergines
- Frozen peas
- Frozen spinach

Extras I love

- Olives
- Edamame beans
- Fresh herbs

- Special cheese (such as taleggio, manchego, burrata, gruyère)
- Chilli peppers

- Lemongrass stalks
- Fresh lemons and limes
- Pomegranate seeds

STORE-CUPBOARD

Basics

- Porridge oats
- Rice (such as pre-cooked, arborio or otherwise)
- Pre-cooked puy lentils and quinoa
- Pasta (such as fusilli, shells, orzo, fresh noodles, dried noodles)
- Tinned beans and pulses (kidney beans, black beans, cannellini beans, chickpeas)
- Quick-cook polenta

- Filo pastry
- Nuts and seeds (such as almonds, walnuts, pine nuts, cashews, pecan nuts, sesame seeds, nigella seeds)
- Tomato puree
- Chopped tomatoes and passata
- Coconut oil
- Olive oil
- Stock (chicken, vegetable, fish)

- Sea salt and black pepper
- Basic spices (such as dried chilli flakes; garam masala; ground turmeric; cayenne pepper; smoked paprika; ground cinnamon, ground cumin; ground coriander)
- Light soy sauce
- Red and white wine vinegar
- Dijon mustard
- Jarred roasted red peppers
- Jarred sundried tomatoes

Extras I love

- Tahini
- Sriracha
- Fish sauce
- Sesame oil
- Miso powder or paste
- Jarred anchovies

- Jarred capers
- Ready-made pastes (such as harissa, chipotle and tikka masala curry)
- Balsamic vinegar
- Rice vinegar

- Special spices (such as star anise; mustard seeds; cardamom pods; fennel seeds; fenugreek seeds; Sichuan peppercorns; dukkah mix; sumac; saffron)

All-day Breakfast

Smashed peas
HAM & EGG MUFFINS

* Serves 2

1 chicken stock cube
300g frozen peas
2 English muffins, cut in half
4 eggs
1 red chilli, finely chopped
3 spring onions, trimmed and finely sliced
1 tbsp coriander, chopped
juice of ½ lime
salt and black pepper
4 thick slices of thick-cut, deli-style ham, visible fat removed

Bring two pans of water to the boil and add the chicken stock cube to one of them. When the stock pan is boiling, drop the frozen peas into the stock and boil for about 8 minutes or until the peas are very tender. Before you drain the peas, scoop out half a mugful of the cooking liquid and keep to one side.

Drain the peas and put your muffins on to toast. Carefully crack your eggs into the hot water, reducing the heat until the water is just 'burping'. Cook the eggs for about 4 minutes for a runny yolk, then carefully lift them out with a slotted spoon and drain on kitchen roll.

Tip the peas back into the pan they were cooked in and add the red chilli, sliced spring onions, coriander and lime juice, along with a splash of the reserved stock and a good pinch of both salt and pepper. Use a hand blender to blitz the peas into a coarse-textured mix – I like it to be smooth in parts, but also quite coarse. Add a little more stock if necessary.

Plate up the hot, toasted muffins and top each one with a slice of ham, a mound of the peas and a perfectly poached egg.

CHEESE, SPINACH & HAM
everyday omelette

* Serves 1

3 eggs
salt and black pepper
knob of butter
large handful of baby
spinach leaves
20g cheddar, grated
75g good-quality ham,
roughly torn
green salad, to serve

Crack the eggs into a bowl and add a tiny sprinkle of salt and a good grind of pepper. Beat the eggs together with a fork.

Heat the butter over a medium to high heat in a small non-stick frying pan. When the butter is bubbling and melted, drop in the spinach and stir to wilt.

As soon as all of the spinach has just wilted, pour in the beaten eggs.

Using a wooden spoon, beat the eggs around the pan as if you are scrambling them. Continue to do this until the mixture starts to resemble very loose scrambled egg. At this point, reduce the heat to low and spread the egg out over the base of the pan.

Sprinkle the cheese over half of the omelette and place the ham on top of the cheese. Turn off the heat.

Give the omelette a poke around the edges to ensure it's set, then, lifting it up by the handle, gently tip the pan away from you and, using your spoon, lift the edge closest to you and roll it over.

Pull out your plate, then tip the omelette onto the plate so that the browned bottom of the omelette becomes the top.

Serve up your classic omelette with a little side salad.

CHOCOLATE MALT
overnight oats

* Serves 4
* Make ahead

55g fat-free Greek yoghurt
3 scoops (90g) chocolate
protein powder
1 scoop (30g) low-sugar
malted-milk drink powder
600ml almond milk
275g porridge oats

To serve
handful of raspberries
handful of roasted hazelnuts,
chopped

Whisk together the yoghurt, protein powder, malted-milk drink powder and almond milk until there are no lumps.

Stir in the porridge oats and leave in a container overnight.

Serve with the raspberries and chopped hazelnuts.

Photo overleaf

GOAT'S CHEESE & CHORIZO
morning muffins

* Makes 12
* Make ahead

2 tsp coconut oil
125g cooking chorizo, cut into
5mm pieces
100g frozen peas
75g soft goat's cheese
8 eggs
salt and black pepper
125g jarred roasted red
peppers, drained and cut
into thin 3cm strips
4 spring onions, trimmed and
finely sliced

Preheat the oven to 190°C (fan 170°C/gas mark 5).

Heat the oil in a small frying pan over a medium heat and add the chorizo pieces. Fry for 3–4 minutes until cooked through, then turn off the heat and leave.

Bring a kettle to the boil. Tip the peas into a bowl, pour the boiling water over the peas and leave to sit for 1 minute. Drain and leave to one side.

Tip the goat's cheese into a bowl and crack in 2 eggs along with a pinch of salt and pepper. Whisk the cheese together with the eggs until fully combined. Whisk in the remaining eggs, then stir in the cooked chorizo along with any of the red cooking oil, the peas, red peppers and spring onions. Mix well.

Equally divide the mixture between the twelve holes of a muffin tin, then slide into the oven and bake for 15 minutes. When cooked, remove and leave to cool.

Masala eggy bread
WITH QUICK TOMATO RELISH

* Serves 2

6 eggs
2 tsp garam masala
2 tsp ground turmeric
½ tsp cayenne pepper
salt and black pepper
4 medium slices of bread
1 tbsp coconut oil
½ tsp brown mustard seeds
2 cloves garlic, finely chopped
½ red onion, peeled and finely diced
3cm ginger, peeled and finely chopped
1 green chilli, finely sliced
½ tsp ground cumin
½ tsp ground coriander
2 large ripe tomatoes, roughly chopped into chunks
handful of fresh coriander, chopped, to serve

Whisk together the eggs with the garam masala, turmeric and cayenne pepper and a good pinch of both salt and pepper. Pour the mix into a baking dish, or something deep and wide. Lay the bread slices in the mix and turn them over a few times to start them soaking well.

Soak the bread for 5–10 minutes, turning every now and again.

Meanwhile, make the relish. Melt half of the oil in a saucepan over a medium to high heat, then add the mustard seeds. Fry for 30 seconds, then add the garlic, onion, ginger and green chilli and fry, stirring regularly, for 4 minutes.

Sprinkle in the cumin and coriander and stir to combine. Slide in the tomatoes and turn the heat down a little (if your tomatoes aren't very ripe, add a splash of water). Cook the relish for 10 minutes, stirring every now and again.

It is likely you will have to cook the eggy bread in two batches. So melt half of the remaining oil in a large non-stick frying pan over a medium to high heat, then cook the bread gently for about 2 minutes on each side. It should be golden brown on the outside and cooked all the way through. Transfer the bread to a piece of kitchen roll to blot off excess oil, then wipe out the pan and repeat the process with the remaining oil and soaked bread.

Serve up the eggy bread with the relish and a sprinkling of chopped coriander.

Cover the leftover relish and keep it in the fridge for up to 5 days.

Baked eggs
IN HERBY MUSHROOMS

8 portobello mushrooms
40ml olive oil
2 cloves garlic, minced
4 sprigs of thyme, leaves only
salt and black pepper
4 big handfuls of baby
spinach leaves
8 eggs
4 tbsp grated parmesan
600g thick-cut, deli-style ham,
to serve

Preheat the oven to 200°C (fan 180°C/gas mark 6).

Take each mushroom one at a time, upturn it and break off the stalk. Using a spoon, scoop out all the brown gills to leave yourself hollowed mushrooms. Line them up, hollowed-out side up, on a flat baking tray.

Mix together the olive oil, garlic and thyme along with a pinch of salt and pepper. Drizzle the garlic and herb mix over the scooped-out side of the mushrooms, then slide the tray into the oven and bake for 10 minutes.

While the mushrooms are baking, tip the spinach into a sieve and bring a full kettle to the boil. When boiled, pour the water over the waiting spinach to wilt it, then immediately cool it with cold running water. Pick up the spinach with both hands and give it a big squeeze to remove as much of the liquid as you can.

After 10 minutes, remove the mushrooms from the oven and lightly rub them with kitchen roll to absorb any liquid that may have been produced.

Give the spinach one last squeeze, then divide it among the eight mushrooms, creating a sort of ring within the scooped-out circle.

Crack an egg into the centre of each spinach-lined mushroom and sprinkle the parmesan over the top. Slide the mushrooms back into the oven and bake for 12 minutes.

While the eggs are baking, heat the ham by placing it on a plate and pouring over a little hot water. Cover it with cling film and zap it in the microwave.

After 12 minutes, the yolks should be just runny. Serve the mushrooms straight up with the warmed ham.

Carrot fritters
WITH EGGS & HALLOUMI

* Serves 2
(makes 4)
* Make ahead
* Freeze ahead

1 small carrot, peeled and
grated (about 110g)

¼ courgette, trimmed and
grated (about 60g)

2 spring onions, trimmed and
finely sliced

30g ground almonds

10g plain flour

3 eggs

salt and black pepper

½ tbsp coconut oil

6 slices of halloumi

sweet chilli sauce, to serve

Mix together the grated carrot and courgette in a bowl along with the sliced spring onions, ground almonds, flour and one of the eggs. Season with a little salt and pepper and then stir everything well with a fork to bring it together. The mixture can appear to be a bit wet – don't be tempted to add extra flour.

Put a pan of water on to boil for your poached eggs.

Melt half of the coconut oil in a large non-stick frying pan over a medium to high heat, then spoon the mixture in, making four roughly equal-sized circles. If you don't have a large enough pan to fry all four at the same time, then fry them in batches.

Fry the fritters for 2–3 minutes on each side, or until they are browned and the egg is cooked all the way through. Transfer the fritters to a piece of kitchen roll to dab off any excess oil.

Carefully crack the remaining eggs into the hot water, reducing the heat until the water is just 'burping'. Cook the eggs for about 4 minutes for a runny yolk, then carefully lift them out with a slotted spoon and drain on kitchen roll.

While the eggs are poaching, wipe out the pan and add the remaining oil. Melt the coconut oil over a medium to high heat, then add the halloumi and fry for about 45 seconds on each side, or until nicely browned and soft in the middle.

Serve up the fritters, laying the halloumi on top, then finish with a poached egg and sweet chilli sauce.

Full English bake-up

* Serves 4

1 tbsp sunflower oil
8 good-quality sausages
or chipolatas
8 rashers of smoked
streaky bacon
2 tomatoes, cut in half
6 large chestnut mushrooms,
roughly halved
4 sprigs of thyme, leaves only
4 eggs

To serve
4 large handfuls of
spinach leaves
brown sauce

Preheat the oven to 210°C (fan 190°C/gas mark 6–7).

Pour the oil onto a flat baking tray and slide into the oven to preheat for 5 minutes. Remove the tray and quickly lay the sausages on, then slide the tray back into the oven and cook for 10 minutes (or 5 minutes if you're using chipolatas).

Slide the tray out of the oven, quickly flip the sausages and then lay the bacon rashers on and around the sausages before sliding the tray back into the oven and cooking for a further 5 minutes.

Remove the tray again and dot around the tomatoes and mushrooms. Sprinkle with the thyme leaves, then slide the tray back into the oven and cook for 10 minutes.

Carefully remove the tray and pour off any excess liquid released by the mushrooms.

Push the cooking ingredients around a little to create four small wells in the mixture. Crack the eggs into the small wells, then slide the tray back into the oven for a final 5 minutes.

Serve with a handful of spinach and some brown sauce.

* This only works with decent-quality ingredients. Cheap bacon will flood your tray with water and give you a 'full poach-up'!

Tahini & yoghurt eggs
WITH CHORIZO

* Serves 2

240g Greek yoghurt
60g tahini
1 fat clove garlic, minced
175g cooking chorizo, cut into
5mm pieces
4 eggs
½ bunch of parsley, roughly
chopped

MAKE IT VEG
Simply drop the chorizo
and add a handful of
pine nuts.

Pour about 5cm of water into a medium pan and bring to the boil. Put another larger pan almost filled to the brim with water on to heat as well – this will be for poaching the eggs.

Tip the yoghurt and tahini into a bowl that sits snugly on top of the medium pan, making sure the base of the bowl does not touch the boiling water. Add the garlic and a little splash of water to loosen the ingredients, then sit the bowl over the steaming pan of water. Leave the ingredients to warm through, stirring every now and again for about 5 minutes, or until just warmed through.

Tip the chorizo pieces into a small non-stick frying pan over a medium heat. As the chorizo warms, it releases oil. Let it fry in this oil until lightly browned and crisp, then take the pan off the heat.

Carefully crack your eggs into the hot water, reducing the heat until the water is just 'burping'. Cook the eggs for about 4 minutes for a runny yolk, then carefully lift them out with a slotted spoon and drain on kitchen roll.

When ready to plate up, give the tahini sauce a stir – it is likely you will have to add a little more warm water to loosen the sauce to the consistency of very thick double cream.

Divide the sauce into two shallow bowls, scoop the eggs onto the sauce, then top with the fried chorizo pieces, drizzling over some of the delicious oil.

Finish with a good covering of chopped parsley and get stuck in.

Chicken

Mexican tortilla
WITH CHICKEN & FETA

* Serves 2
* Make ahead

2 tbsp coconut oil
1 x 250g skinless chicken breast, chopped
2 red onions, peeled and thinly sliced
6 eggs
salt and black pepper
2 large fistfuls of spinach
80g feta
50g tinned sweetcorn, drained
1 avocado, de-stoned and cut into thin wedges
small bunch of coriander, roughly chopped
1 red chilli, finely sliced – remove the seeds if you don't like it hot

Melt half of the coconut oil in a medium non-stick ovenproof frying pan. Slide in the chicken pieces and stir-fry gently for 7 minutes until the chicken is cooked. Check by slicing into it to make sure the meat is white all the way through, with no raw pink bits left. Leave to one side.

Melt the remaining oil in the pan over a medium to high heat. Add the sliced onions and cook for 10 minutes, stirring every now and again until the onions are soft and lightly browned.

Turn on your grill to maximum.

Crack the eggs into a bowl and beat together with a small pinch of salt and pepper. Crank up the heat under the onions to maximum and add the spinach, turning it regularly until wilted.

Pour the beaten eggs into the pan, and as the tortilla sets round the edges, draw the cooked egg into the middle, allowing the centre to be filled with raw egg. Continue to cook your eggs like this until the mix is three-quarters cooked through. Turn the heat off under the pan and crumble the feta evenly over the surface of the egg.

Slide the frying pan under the hot grill. Let the tortilla grill for 2–3 minutes, or until the feta is just starting to brown and there is no raw egg visible on the surface of the tortilla.

Remove the pan from the grill, carefully slide the tortilla onto a chopping board and scatter with the sweetcorn, cooked chicken, avocado, coriander and red chilli. Wedge it up and serve.

Teriyaki ginger chicken
WITH AUBERGINE & RICE

* Serves 4

1 tbsp coconut oil

4 cloves garlic, finely chopped

1 large aubergine, trimmed and cut into 4cm batons (275g)

100ml water

35ml light soy sauce

2cm ginger, peeled and roughly cut into small pieces

1 x 300g chicken breast, cut into 1cm strips

125g oyster mushrooms, large ones, torn in half

600g pre-cooked rice

3 spring onions, trimmed and finely sliced

Melt half of the coconut oil in a saucepan over a medium to high heat, then add the garlic and fry for 30 seconds. Throw in the aubergine on top. Fry the aubergine and garlic together for about 2 minutes, then add the water and soy sauce. Bring the liquid to the boil, cover with a lid and simmer on a low heat for 15 minutes, or until the aubergine pieces have pretty much broken down. Keep half an eye on the water levels – add little splashes of water to the pan if you think it's necessary.

While the aubergine is cooking, heat up the remaining oil in a large frying pan or wok over a high heat, then add the ginger and sliced chicken breast and stir-fry for 2 minutes. Add the mushrooms and continue to stir-fry for 2–3 minutes or until you are happy the chicken is fully cooked through and the mushrooms are just starting to wilt a little.

Heat up your rice in the microwave.

Serve up mounds of rice topped with the tasty aubergine and chicken and sprinkled with the sliced spring onions.

I like using pre-cooked rice, but if you prefer you could cook 200g rice according to packet instructions.

rilled lemon chicken
WITH CAULIFLOWER RICE

* Serves 4
* Make ahead

4 x 200g skinless chicken
breasts
3 tsp fresh oregano leaves,
roughly chopped
3 tsp fresh thyme leaves,
roughly chopped
juice of 1 lemon
4 tbsp olive oil
800g cauliflower florets
(2 caulis)
5 spring onions, trimmed and
finely sliced
1 tsp sweet smoked paprika
½ tsp ground cumin
salt and black pepper
watercress, to serve

Take each chicken breast one at a time and lay lengthways on
your chopping board. Cut into the side of the breast as if you
were trying to cut the breast in half horizontally, but stop about
1cm from slicing all the way through. Open the meat up like
a book and give it a little push with the palm of your hand to
flatten. Place in a large tray and repeat the process with the
remaining chicken.

Sprinkle in the oregano and thyme leaves and add the lemon
juice and 3 tablespoons of the olive oil. Leave the chicken to
sit for 5 minutes.

While the chicken is marinating, blitz up the cauliflower florets
until they resemble couscous.

When you are ready to eat, heat up both a griddle pan and a
large frying pan over a high heat. When the griddle pan is hot,
drain the excess oil from the chicken breasts and griddle on each
side for 3 minutes, by which time they should be fully cooked
through and nicely browned. Check by slicing into the chicken
to make sure the meat is white all the way through, with no
raw pink bits left.

In the large frying pan, heat up the remaining olive oil and when
it is hot, add the spring onions and fry for 30 seconds, then add
the cauliflower and cook, stirring regularly over the high heat for
5 minutes. Sprinkle in the ground spices along with a generous
pinch of salt and pepper, then take off the heat.

Serve up the cauliflower topped with the chicken, and finally
add a good handful of watercress per person.

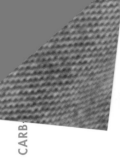

Chicken fried rice

WITH MANGO & BASIL

* Serves 2

½ tbsp coconut oil

4 spring onions, trimmed and finely sliced

2 cloves garlic, finely chopped

1 x 300g skinless chicken breast, cut into 1cm slices

1 small carrot, peeled and diced

5 baby sweetcorn, cut in half lengthways

80g frozen peas

400g pre-cooked rice

1½ tbsp soy sauce

1 tsp sesame oil

1 mango, peeled and cut into rough 2cm cubes

2 red chillies, finely sliced – remove the seeds if you don't like the heat

small bunch of basil, roughly chopped

Melt the coconut oil in a large frying pan or wok over a high heat, then chuck in the spring onions and garlic and fry for 30 seconds. Add the chicken slices and stir-fry for 2 minutes, then add the carrot, sweetcorn and frozen peas. Stir-fry everything together for 3 minutes, by which time the chicken should be just about cooked through.

Add the rice and toss together with the other ingredients. Add a splash of water to the pan, and let it steam up to help separate and warm through the rice and finish off cooking the chicken and vegetables. Fry the rice until you are happy the rice is completely heated through.

Take the mix off the heat and stir through the soy sauce and sesame oil, then, when the sauces are well combined, stir in the mango pieces.

Serve up the rice, topped with the fiery chilli slices and chopped basil.

I like using pre-cooked rice, but if you prefer you could cook 135g rice according to packet instructions and allow to cool before adding to the pan.

Chicken & aubergine 'pizza'

* Serves 2
* Make ahead

2 aubergines
3–4 tbsp olive oil
10g tomato puree
200g chopped tomatoes
1 clove garlic, roughly chopped
½ tsp dried oregano
salt and black pepper
2 x 180g skinless chicken breasts
100g taleggio or mozzarella
rocket, to serve

MAKE IT VEG
Omit the chicken and give the pizza a generous sprinkling of pumpkin seeds, sunflower seeds, cashews or pistachios.

Preheat the oven to 200°C (fan 180°C/gas mark 6).

Cut each aubergine lengthways into 8–10 slices, roughly 5mm thick (doesn't need to be an exact science!).

Heat a large griddle pan over a high heat and drizzle the aubergine slices with a little olive oil. Griddle the aubergine slices in batches, cooking them for about 1 minute on each side – they should be nicely marked by the pan and just cooked through.

While the aubergine slices are cooking, slide the tomato puree, chopped tomatoes, garlic clove and dried oregano into a food processor and blitz until smooth. Season with a little salt and pepper.

Put each chicken breast between two pieces of cling film, and using a rolling pin, lightly beat until slightly thinned to an even thickness. Brush each side with olive oil and cook on the hot griddle pan for 6–8 minutes on each side, until cooked through. Check by slicing into the chicken to make sure the meat is white all the way through, with no raw pink bits left.

Build your pizza by creating a circle, about 20cm in diameter, with some of the aubergine slices, then cover the middle with a few more. Spread over about a third of the tomato sauce, then lay the remaining aubergine slices on top, overlapping them to create a roughly even circle.

Spoon the remaining tomato sauce over the top, lay the cooked chicken on and then dot with taleggio. Bake the 'pizza' in the oven for 10 minutes.

Remove the 'pizza' from the oven, top with rocket and cut into wedges.

Photo overleaf

I love taleggio, so it takes pride of place on top of this pizza, but any cheese – from mozzarella to a blue cheese – would work well. If you decide to make this ahead, simply build your pizza, then leave in the fridge until ready to cook.

JOE'S BANGIN'

chicken balti

* Serves 4
* Make ahead
* Freeze ahead

1½ tbsp coconut oil

2 red onions, peeled and cut into chunks

5 cardamom pods, bruised with the side of a knife

1 stick of cinnamon

4cm ginger, peeled and minced

5 cloves garlic, minced

1 large green chilli, slit down the length

1 red pepper, de-seeded and cut into 3cm chunks

1 green pepper, de-seeded and cut into 3cm chunks

1 tsp ground turmeric

2 tsp garam masala

18 cherry tomatoes, cut in half

150ml water

3 x 200g skinless chicken breasts, cut into large chunks

bunch of coriander, roughly chopped

700g pre-cooked rice

Melt the coconut oil in a large casserole dish over a medium to high heat. Blitz the onions in a food processor until they're pretty much a puree, then tip into the hot, melted oil along with the cardamom pods and the cinnamon stick. Cook for 12 minutes, stirring regularly.

Add the ginger and garlic and cook for a further 2 minutes, then add the chilli, red pepper, green pepper, turmeric and garam masala and cook, stirring regularly, for 2 more minutes.

Crank up the heat a little and chuck in the cherry tomatoes and the water. Bring to the boil, then add the chicken pieces. Simmer the curry for 10 minutes, or until you are sure the chicken is fully cooked through. Check by slicing into one of the larger pieces to make sure the meat is white all the way through, with no raw pink bits left.

Finish the curry with the chopped coriander, and serve with steaming-hot rice.

Do not reduce the onion cooking time because it's pretty much the most important part of cooking. I like using pre-cooked rice, but if you prefer you could cook 235g rice according to packet instructions.

Paprika & lentil stew

WITH HONEY-GLAZED CHICKEN

* Serves 4

1 tbsp coconut oil

1 large onion, peeled and diced

2 sticks of celery, trimmed and diced

100g kale, thick stalks removed

1 fresh bay leaf

1 large fennel bulb, trimmed and diced

3 tomatoes, roughly chopped into 2cm chunks

1½ tsp sweet smoked paprika

275g pre-cooked puy lentils

200ml chicken stock

salt and black pepper

4 x 180–200g chicken breasts

2 stalks of rosemary, needles only, finely chopped

4 tsp honey

Melt half of the coconut oil in a large high-sided frying pan over a medium to high heat, then add the onion. Fry, stirring regularly for about 8 minutes, or until the onions have softened and taken on a little colour.

Add the celery, kale, bay leaf and fennel and continue to fry, stirring every now and again for 4 minutes, then crank up the heat and add the tomatoes, paprika, lentils and stock, along with a good pinch of both salt and pepper. Bring the liquid to the boil, then reduce to a simmer and cook for 10 minutes.

While the stew is cooking, take each breast one at a time and slice into the side, cutting almost all the way through but not quite. Open the breast up like a book and push it with the palm of your hand to flatten it slightly. Repeat the process with the remaining breasts.

Melt the remaining oil in a large non-stick frying pan over a medium to high heat. Season the breasts all over with salt and pepper and sprinkle with the chopped rosemary. When the oil is melted and hot, carefully lay the meat in the hot pan and fry for 4 minutes on one side, then flip and cook for a further 3 minutes, by which time the chicken should be cooked all the way through. Check by slicing into the chicken to make sure the meat is white all the way through, with no raw pink bits left.

Turn the heat off under the pan and pour the honey over the cooked breasts, turning them in the honey to glaze.

Serve the chicken on top of a steaming bowl of the stew.

SINGAPORE
chicken udon noodles

* Serves 2

½ tbsp coconut oil

3 cloves garlic, roughly chopped

2 lemongrass stalks, tender white part only, finely sliced

1 star anise

2 bird's eye chillies, slit lengthways – remove the seeds if you don't like it hot

4cm ginger, peeled and finely chopped

small bunch of coriander, stalks only

6 spring onions, trimmed and finely sliced

2 x 200g skinless chicken breasts, cut into 1cm strips

6 baby sweetcorn, sliced in half

120g mange tout or green beans

400g ready-to-eat udon noodles

1 tbsp mild curry powder

1 tsp ground turmeric

1 chicken stock cube

800ml coconut water

basil, roughly chopped, to serve

Melt the coconut oil in a large, high-sided frying pan or wok over a medium to high heat, then add the garlic, lemongrass, star anise, chillies, ginger, the finely chopped stalks of the coriander and the spring onions. Stir-fry the ingredients for 2 minutes, then turn up the heat and slide in the chicken.

Continue to stir-fry all the ingredients together for 2 minutes, then add the baby sweetcorn, mange tout and udon noodles. Toss everything together for 1 minute.

Sprinkle in the curry powder and the turmeric and toss to incorporate. Crumble in the stock cube and pour in the coconut water. Bring the whole lot to the boil, then sprinkle over the chopped basil.

Divide the soup between two bowls and serve.

* This recipe requires the stalks from a bunch of coriander. Make sure you save the leaves for another recipe.

Chicken tostadas

* Serves 2

4 medium tortillas (about 15cm)
2 tbsp olive oil
2 x 180g skinless chicken breasts
1 large red onion
juice of 2 fat limes
1 baby gem lettuce, trimmed and shredded
¼ cucumber, de-seeded and cut into 1cm pieces
1 red chilli, de-seeded and finely chopped
400g kidney beans, drained and rinsed
½ bunch of coriander, roughly chopped
salt and black pepper

Preheat the oven to 200°C (fan 180°C/gas mark 6).

Lay your tortillas on two flat baking trays, making sure they don't overlap. If using a brush, then brush over the faintest covering of olive oil on one side.

Slide the trays into your oven and bake for 10 minutes, by which time the tortillas will have browned a little and should be nice and crisp. Remove and leave to cool.

While the tostadas are baking, put each chicken breast between two pieces of cling film, and using a rolling pin, lightly beat until slightly thinned to an even thickness. Brush each side with olive oil and cook on a hot griddle pan for 6–8 minutes on each side, until cooked through. Check by slicing into the chicken to make sure the meat is white all the way through, with no raw pink bits left. Leave to one side to cool, then chop into 1cm strips.

Mix together all of the remaining ingredients with the cooked chicken and season with a little salt and pepper.

Overlap two tostadas on each plate and pile up the topping.

* You could use an oil-spray bottle to give the tortillas the faintest covering of oil before they are baked. Just give each tortilla a couple of pumps on one side.

CHICKEN & MUSHROOM
risotto

* Serves 4
* Make ahead
* Freeze ahead

12g dried porcini mushrooms
2 chicken stock cubes
1 tbsp coconut oil
1 large leek, trimmed, washed and finely chopped
5 sprigs of thyme
400g skinless and boneless chicken thighs, cut into 2cm pieces
300g mushrooms, brushed clean and roughly chopped into 2cm chunks
225g arborio rice
small bunch of parsley, roughly chopped
small bunch of chives, finely chopped
juice of 1 lemon
salt and black pepper

Pour enough boiling water over the dried mushrooms to cover them generously, then leave to soak. Drop the stock cubes into a jug and, using boiling water, make up 750ml of stock.

Melt half of the oil in a large saucepan over a medium to high heat, then slide in the leek and thyme. Stir and cook for 2 minutes, then cover and leave to sweat for 2 minutes.

Take the lid off and crank up the heat to maximum. Add the chicken thigh pieces and a third of the chopped mushrooms. Cook, stirring every now and again, for 2 minutes. Slide in the rice and stir in to combine with the other ingredients.

Drain the sodden mushrooms and leave to one side, measuring out 150ml of the liquid. Pour the liquid into the pan with the sodden mushrooms and allow it to bubble up.

For the next 20 minutes, add a ladleful of the stock at a time to the rice, while constantly stirring. Don't add too much stock to the pan otherwise you will lower the heat, which increases the cooking time. After 20 minutes you should have incorporated all of the stock into the pan, and you should be looking down at a creamy risotto – the rice should be just soft to the bite.

Put a lid on and leave the risotto to sit for a couple of minutes.

Meanwhile, melt the remaining oil in a large frying pan over a high heat, then add the remaining mushrooms. Fry without turning for 1 minute to caramelize.

Add the mushrooms to the risotto along with the chopped parsley, chives and lemon juice. Stir, taste for seasoning then serve.

CHICKEN & SAFFRON

ragu

* Serves 4
* Make ahead
* Freeze ahead

½ tbsp coconut oil

1 large red onion, peeled and diced

3 cloves garlic, finely chopped

5 sprigs of thyme

6 boneless and skinless chicken thighs (600g), each cut into 4 large chunks

300g wholemeal fusilli pasta

8g tomato puree

small pinch of saffron

75ml red wine

250ml passata

large bunch of basil, roughly chopped

50g pitted black olives, roughly chopped

Put a large pan of water on to boil.

Melt the oil in a large, high-sided frying pan over a medium to high heat, and when it is melted and hot, add the red onion, garlic and thyme and fry, stirring regularly for 5 minutes until the onions have softened.

Crank up the heat to maximum and add the chopped chicken thighs to the pan. Without letting the other ingredients burn, try not to stir the meat too much so that it has the chance to brown a little in places. Cook the chicken for about 2 minutes – your aim here is not to cook it through.

This is probably a good time to drop the pasta into the boiling water to cook.

Squeeze in the tomato puree, add the saffron and mix the whole lot together, frying and stirring for about 1 minute.

Pour in the wine and let it bubble, then add the passata and bring it up to a simmer. Cook the ragu like this for about 10 minutes, or until you are happy the chicken is fully cooked through. Check by slicing into the chicken to make sure the meat is white all the way through, with no raw pink bits left.

If you feel the pan is cooking dry, then just scoop out a little of the pasta cooking water and add to the pan.

When the pasta is done and you're happy the chicken is cooked through, drain the pasta then tip it straight into the pan with the sauce.

Add the basil and olives and stir to combine everything.

HARISSA & RED PEPPER
roast chicken

* Serves 4
* Longer recipe
* Make ahead

1 tbsp coconut oil

8 chicken thighs, bone-in and skin-on

1½ tbsp harissa paste

2 fennel bulbs, trimmed and cut into chunky lengths

2 red onions, peeled and cut into wedges

2 red peppers, de-seeded and cut into 3cm chunks

6 tbsp yoghurt

1 tbsp chives, chopped

½ small bunch of parsley, roughly chopped

salt and black pepper

steamed greens, to serve

Preheat the oven to 200°C (fan 180°C/gas mark 6).

Dollop the coconut oil into a heavy-based roasting tray and slide into the oven to melt for 5 minutes.

Tip the chicken thighs into a bowl and spoon over the harissa. Get your hands stuck in and smear the meat all over with the hot paste.

After 5 minutes, slide the tray out and carefully lay the chicken thighs in the hot fat, skin-side down. Tumble all the prepped veg over the top of the chicken, then slide the tray back into the oven. The tray should be crammed with ingredients. Roast for 30 minutes.

After 30 minutes, using a couple of forks or tongs carefully pull the chicken from under the veg and place it on top, skin-side up. Repeat the process with all of the chicken thighs, then slide the tray back into the oven and roast for a further 25 minutes, until you have a tray of lovely caramelized chicken on top of tender vegetables.

Mix together the yoghurt, chives and parsley along with a good pinch of both salt and pepper.

Serve up the chicken and veg with steamed greens and a dollop of the herby yoghurt.

Chicken & miso
NOODLE SOUP

* Serves 2

1 sachet of miso powder
or paste

½ tbsp coconut oil

2 cloves garlic, finely chopped

3cm ginger, peeled and finely
chopped

1 x 300g skinless chicken
breast, cut into 1cm slices

150g oyster mushrooms, large
ones, torn in half

2 pak choy, cut into 4 pieces
lengthways

300g fresh egg noodles

2 small handfuls of bean sprouts

2 spring onions, finely sliced

1½ tbsp light soy sauce

Bring a kettle to the boil and dilute the miso powder or paste with 500ml of boiling water. Leave to one side.

Melt the oil in a large frying pan or wok over a medium to high heat, then add the garlic and ginger and stir-fry for 30 seconds. Add the chicken and continue to stir-fry the ingredients together for 3 minutes. Add the mushrooms and pak choy. Fry all together for 2–3 minutes, or until the chicken and the mushrooms are lightly browned and virtually cooked through.

Drop the noodles in and give them a toss together with all the other cooking ingredients.

Turn down the heat a little and pour in the miso. Slowly bring the liquid up to the boil and simmer for 1 minute.

Serve up the noodles topped with the bean sprouts, spring onions and the soy sauce.

MAKE IT VEG
Replace the chicken with the same quantity of tofu, either silken or firm. Simply chuck it in with the miso and simmer for 5 minutes.

Paprika chicken

WITH APPLE & DILL SLAW

* Serves 4

2 tbsp olive oil

2 tsp sweet smoked paprika

1 tsp onion granules

1 tsp celery salt

12 skinless and boneless chicken thighs

½ small red cabbage (300g), core removed

1 carrot, peeled and cut into matchsticks (100g)

1 apple, peeled and cored and cut into matchsticks (100g)

small bunch of dill, finely chopped

4 spring onions, trimmed and finely chopped

75g mayonnaise

60g pecans, roughly chopped

Preheat the oven to 200°C (fan 180°C/gas mark 6).

Pour the oil into a large sandwich bag and add the paprika, onion granules and celery salt. Mix together, then add the chicken thighs, seal the bag and give the whole lot a good squidge around to ensure the chicken is evenly coated in the spiced oil.

Tip the thighs onto a baking tray and roast in the oven for 25 minutes, or until you are certain the chicken is fully cooked through. You can check by slicing into one of the larger pieces to make sure the meat is white all the way through, with no raw pink bits left.

While the chicken is cooking, mix together all the remaining ingredients to make a tasty coleslaw.

Serve up the chicken on top of a pile of coleslaw.

* You can make the slaw ahead, but squeeze it with a little lemon juice to stop the apple from browning.

CHICKEN & ORZO
rat-a-tat bake

* Serves 4
* Make ahead
* Freeze ahead

1 tbsp coconut oil

1 red onion, peeled and diced

1 courgette, trimmed and diced (250g)

1 aubergine, trimmed and diced (250g)

4 sprigs of fresh oregano

4 sprigs of fresh thyme

3 cloves garlic, finely chopped

1 tbsp tomato puree

250g orzo

1 x 400g tin of chopped tomatoes

250ml chicken stock

2 x 200g chicken breasts, cut into 1cm slices

1 tsp sweet smoked paprika

salt and black pepper

small bunch of parsley, roughly chopped

small bunch of chives, finely chopped

Preheat the oven to 200°C (fan 180°C/gas mark 6).

Melt half of the oil in a heavy-based flameproof casserole dish over a medium to high heat. Add the onion and cook for 1 minute, then throw in the courgette, aubergine, oregano, thyme and 2 chopped garlic cloves. Fry, stirring regularly for 5 minutes, until the vegetables are starting to soften.

Add the tomato puree and orzo and mix to combine. Pour in the chopped tomatoes and chicken stock and bring the mixture quickly to the boil, stirring regularly. Put the lid on and slide the dish into the oven.

Meanwhile, melt the remaining oil in a large frying pan over a high heat. Add the sliced chicken and the remaining chopped garlic clove. Stir-fry the chicken so that it is virtually cooked through – it is more important at this stage to colour the meat than to cook it through.

Sprinkle in the paprika along with a pinch of salt and pepper and toss the whole lot together.

Remove the pasta from the oven and carefully take off the lid, stir in the chicken, slide the lid back on and bake the whole lot together for 10 more minutes.

After 10 minutes, take the dish from the oven and stir through the parsley and chives. Serve straight from the dish to the masses.

WEST COAST QUINOA
chicken bowl

* Serves 2
* Make ahead

1 x 300g skinless chicken breast

2–3 tsp olive oil

250g pre-cooked quinoa – red and white mixed

1 x 400g tin of black beans, drained and rinsed

2 tbsp pomegranate molasses

1½ tbsp white wine vinegar

3 spring onions, trimmed and finely sliced

¼ small red cabbage, shredded

16 cherries, de-stoned and halved

1 carrot, peeled and grated

small bunch of coriander, to serve

Put the chicken breast between two pieces of cling film, and using a rolling pin, lightly beat until slightly thinned to an even thickness. Brush each side with olive oil and cook on a hot griddle pan for 6–8 minutes on each side, until cooked through. Check by slicing into the chicken to make sure the meat is white all the way through, with no raw pink bits left.

Ping the quinoa in the microwave according to the packet instructions, then tip into a bowl and stir through the beans immediately. Leave to sit.

Mix together the pomegranate molasses with the vinegar and keep to one side. Shred the chicken breast.

Stir the sliced spring onions and half of the molasses dressing through the warm quinoa and bean mix, then divide between two bowls. Top the bowls with the cabbage, cherries, carrot and shredded chicken, then drizzle over the remaining dressing.

Finish with a scattering of chopped coriander.

GRIDDLED
Caesar Niçoise

* Serves 2

4 large spring onions,
each trimmed and cut
into 3 long batons

8 midget trees (tenderstem
broccoli), cut in half lengthways

80g green beans, trimmed

20ml olive oil

salt and black pepper

2 x 180–200g chicken breasts

3 sprigs of thyme, leaves only

1 lemon

60g mayonnaise

10g jarred anchovies, drained
and roughly chopped

15g parmesan, grated

2 baby gem lettuces, leaves
separated

50g pitted black olives (I like
the slightly dried Crespo ones
for this)

Put a large griddle pan on to heat over a high flame and fling open some windows – this could get a bit smoky.

Put the spring onions, midget trees and green beans into a bowl and pour in half of the olive oil, along with a good pinch of salt and pepper. Toss the ingredients in the oil to season, then when the griddle is hot, carefully lay on the slicked vegetables and cook, turning regularly for 6 minutes, or until just cooked through. Remove and keep to one side.

While the vegetables are cooking, take each chicken breast one at a time and slice into the thick side, cutting almost but not all the way through. Open the breast up like a book and push down on it with the palm of your hand to flatten the meat a little. Place the prepared chicken breast in a bowl and repeat the process with the second breast.

Pour the remaining oil over the chicken breasts and add the thyme leaves, the juice of half of the lemon and a good pinch of salt, then roughly swish the meat around the bowl to coat it with the flavours.

→

GRIDDLED

Caesar Niçoise

(continued)

When the griddle is clear of the veg, lay the breasts on and griddle for 3–4 minutes on each side, or until you are sure the meat is cooked through. Check by slicing into one of the thicker pieces to make sure the meat is white all the way through, with no raw pink bits left. Remove the chicken to a plate and leave to rest a little.

Blitz the mayonnaise, anchovies, parmesan and the juice of the remaining lemon half until smooth. (Depending on how much juice comes from the lemon, you may or may not need to add a splash of water to the dressing.)

Divide the salad leaves over two plates, then arrange the cooked veg over the top. Slice the chicken into strips and add to the plates. Finish with a few black olives and a good drizzling of the dressing.

You can make all the salad components ahead, then toss them together just before serving.

FENNEL & RADISH
chicken noodles

* Serves 2

½ tbsp coconut oil

1 large fennel bulb, trimmed and finely sliced

8 radishes, trimmed and finely sliced

4 spring onions, trimmed and finely sliced

3 cloves garlic, finely sliced

2 x 180g chicken breasts, cut into 1cm strips

4 baby sweetcorn, cut into thin rounds

300g fresh egg noodles

1½ tbsp light soy sauce

Melt the coconut oil in a large frying pan over a medium to high heat, then chuck in the fennel and radishes and stir-fry for 2 minutes.

Add the spring onions and garlic and continue to stir-fry for a further minute.

Crank up the heat to maximum, then slide in the chicken pieces and stir-fry for about 3 minutes. Check by slicing into one of the pieces to make sure the meat is white all the way through, with no raw pink bits left. If you feel the ingredients are burning before the chicken is cooked, pour in about 2 tablespoons of water and let it steam up.

Add the sweetcorn and noodles and toss to mix all the ingredients together. Add a couple more tablespoons of water to warm the noodles.

Turn the heat off, stir through the soy sauce and serve up.

CHICKEN & SQUID
orzo paella

* Serves 4
* Make ahead
* Freeze ahead

1 chicken stock cube
pinch of saffron
1½ tbsp coconut oil
2 red onions, peeled and diced
1 red pepper, de-seeded and
cut into thin slices
3 cloves garlic, chopped
5 medium tomatoes (320g),
roughly chopped
10g tomato puree
300g orzo
¼ tsp smoked paprika
125g frozen peas
300g baby squid, cleaned
and prepped
2 x 200g chicken breasts, cut
into 1cm-thick slices
large bunch of parsley, roughly
chopped
2 lemons, cut into quarters,
to serve

Put a kettle on to boil and preheat the oven to 200°C (fan
180°C/gas mark 6).

Pour 500ml boiling water over the chicken stock cube and add
the saffron. Leave to steep.

Melt 1 tablespoon of the coconut oil over a high heat in a
large ovenproof pan or flameproof casserole dish, then add the
chopped onions, red pepper and garlic and stir-fry for 5 minutes.

Stir in the fresh tomatoes and the tomato puree and continue to
stir-fry for a further 5 minutes, until the tomatoes begin to break
down. Stir in the orzo, paprika and frozen peas, and finally pour
in the infused chicken stock along with the bits of saffron. Bring
the liquid to the boil, clamp on a lid and slide the pan or dish
into the oven. Bake for 15 minutes.

While the orzo is cooking, take the baby squid tubes and cut
them in half lengthways. Score the inside of the flesh at 5mm
intervals in one direction, then turn 45 degrees and score
again to create a diamond pattern. Repeat the scoring with the
remaining squid.

->

* It's not totally necessary to score the squid,
  but it looks good and helps to keep it tender.

CHICKEN & SQUID

orzo paella

(continued)

Melt half of the remaining coconut oil in a large frying pan over a high heat, then fry the chicken for about 4 minutes or until you are happy it's totally cooked through. Try not to stir the meat too much to allow it to brown.

Scrape the chicken out of the pan into a waiting bowl, wipe the frying pan with a piece of kitchen roll and place straight back onto the heat with the remaining coconut oil. Melt the oil until it is blisteringly hot, then carefully add the squid and stir-fry for about 2 minutes, or until just cooked through.

Remove the paella from the oven, carefully take off the lid then top with the fried chicken and squid. Finish with a generous scattering of chopped parsley and lemon wedges.

Chicken & brussels

WITH PASTA SHELLS

* Serves 2

200g pasta shells
½ tbsp coconut oil
pinch of dried chilli flakes
zest and juice of 1 lemon
4 cloves garlic, finely chopped
1 fresh red chilli, finely sliced –
remove the seeds if you don't
like it hot
1 x 300g chicken breast, cut into
1cm slices
250g brussels sprouts, trimmed
and shredded
salt and black pepper
bunch of parsley, roughly
chopped

Put a large pot of water on to boil, and when boiling, cook your pasta according to packet instructions. Just before draining the pasta, scoop out half a mugful of the starchy cooking liquid and keep to one side.

While the pasta is cooking, melt the coconut oil in a large frying pan over a medium to high heat. When the oil is melted and hot, add the chilli flakes, zest of lemon, garlic and fresh chilli. Fry, stirring regularly for 2 minutes, then add the chicken pieces and the brussels sprouts and crank up the heat to maximum. Stir-fry the ingredients all together for about 6 minutes, by which time the brussels should be lightly browned and the chicken pretty much cooked through. Reduce the heat to very low.

Having scooped out some of the water, drain the pasta through a colander then tip into the pan with the chicken. Splash in some of the cooking liquid then add the lemon juice, a good pinch of salt and pepper and the parsley. Toss the whole lot together and enjoy.

BANG BANG
chicken stir-fry

* Serves 4

1 tbsp coconut oil

2 star anise

3 cloves garlic, finely chopped

6 spring onions, trimmed and finely sliced

1 tsp Sichuan peppercorns

3 x 200g chicken breasts, cut into 1cm slices

4 pak choy, cut into quarters lengthways

200g midget trees (tenderstem broccoli), cut in half lengthways

120g baby sweetcorn, cut in half lengthways

500g fresh egg noodles

½ tsp hot smoked paprika

½ tbsp light soy sauce

Melt the oil in a large frying pan or wok over a high heat. Add the star anise and fry for a few seconds, then quickly follow with the garlic, spring onions and Sichuan peppercorns. Stir-fry for 30 seconds.

Tip in the chicken, stirring every now and again so that the meat browns a little, about 2 minutes. Add the pak choy and midget trees and stir-fry for about 3 minutes. Add 2 tablespoons of water to the pan to steam up and cook everything through.

Add the sweetcorn and egg noodles and continue to stir-fry for a couple more minutes until everything is steaming hot.

Take the pan off the heat and add the paprika and soy sauce, tossing the whole lot together to ensure even coverage.

Divide between four plates and enjoy.

Watermelon & chicken
WITH GLASS NOODLES

* Serves 4
* Make ahead

4 x 180–200g skinless
chicken breasts

½ tbsp coconut oil

3 cloves garlic, roughly chopped

2 lemongrass stalks, tender
white part only, finely chopped

2 red chillies, de-seeded and
finely chopped

2 kaffir lime leaves

2 large, very ripe tomatoes,
chopped into 2cm chunks

600g fresh glass noodles
(sometimes called vermicelli)

¼ cucumber, de-seeded and cut
into half-moons

4 spring onions, trimmed and
finely sliced

2 tbsp fish sauce

juice of 3 limes

½ small watermelon, flesh
only, cut into large chunks
(roughly 500g)

bunch of coriander, roughly
chopped

Bring a large pan of water to the boil. When the water is bubbling, gently lay the chicken breasts in the pan and turn the heat down to its lowest setting. Cook the chicken very gently for 12 minutes, then turn the heat off and leave the breasts to sit in the water to keep warm until you're ready to eat.

Melt the coconut oil in a saucepan over a medium to low heat, then add the garlic, lemongrass, chillies, lime leaves and tomatoes. Cook the ingredients slowly for 10 minutes until the tomatoes start to break down a little.

While the chicken and sauce are cooking, bring a kettle to the boil, drop the noodles into a sieve and pour the hot water over the noodles. Follow the hot water with cold water to cool the noodles back down again. Tip the noodles into a large bowl.

Turn the heat off under the tomato pan, then add the cucumber, spring onions, fish sauce and lime juice. Stir to combine everything.

Chuck the tomato dressing into the noodles along with the watermelon pieces. Carefully remove the chicken from the hot water, and using a combination of two forks, shred the meat into small pieces and add these to the large bowl, too.

Add half of the chopped coriander and toss everything gently together.

Serve up the salad sprinkled with the remaining coriander.

Chicken, kale & brussels

* Serves 4

½ tbsp coconut oil

1 onion, peeled and diced

75g smoked streaky bacon, cut into 1cm strips

1 x 300g skinless chicken breast, cut into 1cm strips

190g brussels sprouts, trimmed and shredded

50g kale, thick stalks removed

100g pre-cooked chestnuts, crumbled

80g taleggio or mozzarella

2 red chillies, de-seeded and finely sliced

Melt the coconut oil in a large frying pan over a medium to high heat, then add the onion and chopped bacon. Fry for 2–3 minutes until the bacon is browned and crisp. Slide in the chicken breast and cook for about 4 minutes until it is just cooked through.

Add the brussels and the kale and crank up the heat to maximum. Stir-fry the whole lot together for 2 minutes, then add a splash of water, which will steam up and help to cook the chicken and greens.

Turn on your grill to maximum.

Take the mix off the heat and scatter with the chestnut pieces. Cut the taleggio into rough slices and dot all over. Slide under the hot grill and cook for 2 minutes until the taleggio is just melted.

Finish with a sprinkling of red chilli and serve up.

LIME & CHORIZO

chicken legs

* Serves 4
* Make ahead
* Freeze ahead

12 chicken drumsticks
drizzle of olive oil
salt and black pepper
30g honey
3 limes
20ml soy sauce
8 small cooking chorizo
4 baby gem lettuces, cut in
quarters lengthways
8 radishes, thinly sliced
50g toasted cashews, roughly
chopped

Preheat the oven to 200°C (fan 180°C/gas mark 6).

Tumble the chicken legs into a roasting tray, drizzle over a little oil and sprinkle with salt and pepper. Slide straight into the hot oven and cook for 15 minutes.

Meanwhile, mix together the honey, juice of three limes and the zest of one and the soy sauce in a bowl.

After 15 minutes take the roasting tray out of the oven and add the chorizo. Pour over the lime dressing and toss the whole lot together. Put the tray back into the oven and cook for a further 15 minutes.

After 15 minutes, everything should be nicely cooked through. You can check the chicken by slicing into one of the drumsticks to make sure the meat is white all the way through, with no raw pink bits left.

Serve up the baby gem lettuce, top with the chicken and chorizo and spoon over some of the cooking juices.

Finish with the sliced radish and cashews.

Photo overleaf

Dukkah-spiced chicken
WITH GIANT COUSCOUS & POMEGRANATE DRESSING

* Serves 4
* Make ahead

250g giant couscous
4 x 180–200g skinless
chicken breasts
100g dukkah mix
1 tbsp coconut oil
5 radishes, roughly chopped
½ cucumber, de-seeded and cut
into half-moons
1 jarred red pepper, drained
and cut into 2cm strips
½ red onion, peeled and
finely diced
bunch of parsley, roughly
chopped
2½ tbsp pomegranate molasses
1½ tbsp white wine vinegar
pomegranate seeds,
to serve – optional

Bring a large pot of water to the boil and cook the couscous according to packet instructions. Drain through a sieve and cool down with cold running water. Give it a shake to drain well and tip it into a large bowl.

While the couscous is cooking, take each chicken breast one at a time and slice into the thick side, cutting almost but not all the way through. Open the breast up like a book and push down on it with the palm of your hand to flatten the meat a little. Place the prepared chicken breast in a bowl and repeat the process with the remaining breasts.

Scatter the dukkah onto a plate and then, taking one breast at a time, push it into the mix, sticking as much of the mix to the flesh as you can. Repeat the process with the remaining breasts.

It is likely you will have to cook the breasts two at a time, so melt half of the coconut oil in a large non-stick frying pan over a medium to high heat. Gently lay the two breasts into the hot fat and fry for 3–4 minutes on each side until the chicken is just cooked through. Check by slicing into one of the thicker pieces to make sure the meat is white all the way through, with no raw pink bits left.

Take the chicken from the pan and lightly rub it with kitchen roll, then wipe the pan out and repeat the process with the remaining oil and chicken breasts.

Add the radishes, cucumber, red pepper, red onion and parsley to the couscous. Mix the pomegranate molasses together with the vinegar, then toss the dressing through the couscous salad.

Serve up the couscous with the spiced chicken and a scattering of pomegranate seeds (if using).

BACON-WRAPPED, CHEESE-STUFFED
chicken breasts

* Serves 4

4 × 200g chicken breasts

170g garlic and herb cheese
(I use Le Roule)

12 rashers of smoked streaky
bacon

½ tbsp coconut oil

3 baby gem lettuces, quartered
lengthways

2 avocados, de-stoned and
cut into wedges

16 cherry tomatoes, sliced
in half

salt and black pepper

1 tbsp balsamic vinegar

1 tbsp olive oil

Preheat the oven to 200°C (fan 180°C/gas mark 6).

Take each breast in turn and cut down the entire length of the
breast, ensuring you don't cut all the way through. Using a short
scoring motion, open up the sides a little to create a pocket
shape. Repeat the process with the other chicken breasts.

Spread a quarter of the cheese into the pocket you've created in
each of the chicken breasts, trying to keep it as even as possible.
Gently squeeze the flesh together, then wrap each of the breasts
in three rashers of bacon, keeping the rashers tight without
overlapping them.

Melt the coconut oil in a large ovenproof frying pan over a
medium to high heat, then gently place the breasts in, join-side
down. Fry the breasts for about 3 minutes on each side or until
the bacon has turned a nice brown colour. Slide the pan into
your oven and cook for 15 minutes or until you are happy the
chicken is cooked all the way through – you can check this by
cutting into the thickest part of the breast and ensuring the meat
has turned white, with no raw pink bits left.

While the chicken is cooking, toss together the baby gem
wedges, sliced avocados and cherry tomatoes. Season with a
little salt and pepper, then add the balsamic vinegar and olive oil
and toss gently again.

Divide the salad between four plates and top with the cooked
chicken breasts.

Chipotle chicken
ORANGE & WATERCRESS SALAD

* Serves 2

1½ tbsp coconut oil
6 chicken thighs, bone-in and skin-on
2½ tbsp chipotle paste
salt
1 large red onion, peeled and cut into 12 wedges
1 orange
2 large handfuls of watercress
a couple of drizzles of olive oil
40g walnuts, roughly chopped

Preheat the oven to 220°C (fan 200°C/gas mark 7). Dollop the coconut oil onto a roasting tray and slide into the oven to melt and heat up for 5 minutes.

Place the chicken thighs in a bowl and spoon on the chipotle paste. Give the meat a good swoosh around to evenly coat the thighs. Season generously with salt.

Remove the tray from the oven and quickly but carefully lay the thighs in the hot fat, skin-side down. Tumble the red onion wedges around the chicken and roast the whole lot together for 15 minutes.

Remove the tray and flip the thighs up the other way round and roast for a final 10 minutes.

While the thighs are roasting, peel the orange and cut into slices across its diameter, each slice just thicker than a pound coin.

Serve up the watercress, nestling in the orange slices, and drizzle with a little olive oil. Pile up the chicken thighs, then scatter with the chopped walnuts.

* You can make all the components ahead, then assemble them just before serving.

Roast chicken
WITH BUTTERNUT, FIGS & GOAT'S CHEESE

* Serves 4

1 tbsp coconut oil
1 medium butternut squash, peeled, de-seeded and cut into 2cm cubes (425g)
4 sprigs of thyme, leaves only
4 x 180g chicken breasts, skin-on
6 figs, quartered lengthways
75g soft goat's cheese
40g walnuts, roughly chopped
drizzle of balsamic vinegar
4 handfuls of rocket

Preheat the oven to 210°C (fan 190°C/gas mark 6–7).

Dollop half of the coconut oil onto a baking tray. Drop the chopped butternut squash onto the tray, toss through the thyme leaves then slide the tray into the oven to roast for 20 minutes.

In the meantime, melt the remaining oil in a frying pan over a medium heat, then lay the chicken breasts in the pan, skin-side down. Fry the chicken breasts for about 7 minutes only on the skin side, by which time they should be dark brown. Flip over and cook for a couple of minutes on the other side.

Take your roasting squash from the oven and give it a toss. Lay the chicken on top of the butternut cubes, skin-side up. Dot around the fig quarters and then slide the tray back into your hot oven for a final 10-minute blast.

The chicken should be perfectly cooked through. Check by slicing into one of the thicker pieces of breast to make sure the meat is white all the way through, with no raw pink bits left.

Plate up the chicken, butternut and figs, dot with goat's cheese, then sprinkle over the chopped walnuts and a drizzle of balsamic. Serve with rocket.

* You can make all the components ahead, then assemble them just before serving.

Fish & Seafood

EDAMAME, PINK GINGER &
smoked salmon salad

* Serves 2

150g podded edamame beans
(400g un-podded)

1 courgette, trimmed and
washed

6 radishes, finely sliced

20g pickled pink ginger, drained
and roughly chopped

2 tsp sesame oil

4 tsp rice wine vinegar

2 tsp light soy sauce

225g smoked salmon

black sesame seeds, to serve

Tip the edamame beans into a bowl. Take your courgette and, using a peeler, create long thin ribbons along the entire length of the courgette. When you get close to the core, rotate the courgette and continue on the other side. You won't be able to make ribbons with the whole courgette, so just keep what's left of the core for another recipe, such as a stir-fry.

Add the courgette strips to the edamame along with the sliced radishes.

Mix together the pickled ginger, sesame oil, vinegar and soy sauce in a bowl and pour it over the vegetables. Give the whole lot a toss together, then stack up over two plates. Top with the smoked salmon and sprinkle with black sesame seeds.

Tuna & egg bruschetta

* Serves 2

180g green beans, trimmed
4 slices of thick crusty bread
drizzle of olive oil
1 fat clove garlic
1 large, very ripe tomato, cut in half
2 tsp coconut oil
2 × 140g tuna steaks
salt and black pepper
9 pitted black olives, cut in half
5 sundried tomatoes, drained and patted dry
2 hard-boiled eggs

Bring a pot of water to the boil and when simmering, cook the beans for 3 minutes, or until just cooked through. Drain and leave to one side.

Drizzle the bread with a little olive oil on both sides. Heat a grill over a high heat, and when smoking hot, lay the bread down carefully and cook for 2 minutes on each side until crisp and dark golden.

Remove the bread and immediately rub with the garlic. The bread's rough surface acts as a grater, which wears the garlic down into the bread. Do the same with the tomato, pushing and smudging it into the bread. Leave the bread to one side.

Melt the oil in a frying pan over a high heat. Season the tuna steaks with salt and pepper and carefully lay them in the hot oil. Fry for about 90 seconds on each side, then remove to a plate.

Mix the beans with the olives, sundried tomatoes and a splash of olive oil. Toss together, seasoning as you go.

Slice the tuna into strips. Pile the beans on top of the bread, slice up the eggs and arrange them on top of the beans, then finish with the tuna strips.

** This is a classic breakfast in Spain.
The key is to use good bread and slightly overripe tomatoes.*

Shallot & fennel

WITH GRILLED SEA BASS

* Serves 2

50ml olive oil
1 tsp fennel seeds
3 banana shallots, peeled and sliced finely lengthways (150g)
2 fennel bulbs, trimmed and finely sliced
75ml white wine
4 x 100g sea bass fillets
1 lemon
pea shoots, to serve

You'll need a medium saucepan with a tight-fitting lid for this. Heat the oil in the medium saucepan over a medium to high heat. When the oil is hot, add the fennel seeds and fry for about 30 seconds, then add the shallots and fennel. Crank up the heat to maximum and fry the vegetables for 3 minutes, stirring frequently.

Pour in the wine, allowing it to steam up, then turn down the heat to medium and clamp on a lid. Cook the fennel and shallots, stirring intermittently for 20 minutes, by which time they will be lightly browned but also meltingly tender.

While the veg is stewing, heat the grill to its highest setting. Using a sharp knife, make about four cuts in the skin of the sea bass then sprinkle liberally with salt. Lay the fillets, skin-side up, on a flat tray and cook on the skin side only for 6 minutes, by which time the fish will be cooked through and the skin crisp and slightly blistered in places. Turn off the heat and shut the grill door.

Just before serving, squeeze half a lemon's worth of juice into the fennel and shallots and stir through. Serve up mounds of the fennel and shallots, topped with the fish fillets, a handful of pea shoots and a wedge of lemon.

Sambal sea bass
WITH BAKED COCONUT RICE

* Serves 4

½ tbsp coconut oil

5 large shallots, peeled and diced

7 cloves garlic, roughly chopped

4 cardamom pods, bruised with the side of a knife

275g basmati or jasmine rice

1 chicken stock cube

500ml coconut water

7cm ginger, peeled and roughly chopped

2 lemongrass stalks, tender white part only, finely sliced

1 tbsp fish sauce

5 red chillies, roughly chopped – remove the seeds if you don't like it hot

juice of 1 lime

8 x 100g skinless sea bass fillets

coriander, to serve

Preheat the oven to 190°C (fan 170°C/gas mark 5).

Melt the coconut oil in a large flameproof casserole dish over a medium to high heat, then add 2 diced shallots, 1 clove of chopped garlic and the cardamom pods and fry for 2 minutes.

Tip in the rice and stir to mix with the other ingredients, then crumble in the stock cube. Pour in the coconut water and bring to a boil. Put a lid on the pan and slide it into your hot oven. Bake for 15 minutes.

While the rice is cooking, blitz together the remaining shallots, garlic, ginger, lemongrass, fish sauce, chillies and lime juice. You might have to add a little water to get them started. Smother the sea bass with all but about 3 tablespoons of the sauce. You aren't looking to totally cover the fish, just roughly coat it.

Lay the fish carefully on a baking tray lined with baking parchment, then cook under a hot grill for 5 minutes without turning. The marinade and fish may darken in places, but don't worry.

As soon as the rice and fish are cooked, serve them with a dollop of the reserved sambal sauce and sprigs of coriander.

Tandoori cod burgers
WITH SWEET POTATO FRIES

* Serves 2

2 large sweet potatoes (600g), scrubbed clean
2 tsp olive oil
salt and black pepper
40ml rice vinegar
2g caster sugar
1 red chilli, de-seeded and finely sliced
¼ red onion, finely sliced
¼ cucumber (80g), de-seeded and cut into thin half-moons
2 x 200g skinless and boneless cod fillets
30g tikka masala curry paste
2 burger buns

To serve
1 tbsp fat-free Greek yoghurt
1 tomato, thinly sliced
1 tbsp coriander, chopped

Preheat the oven to 200°C (fan 180°C/gas mark 6).

Cut each sweet potato in half lengthways, then cut into eight long, thin wedges and scatter over one layer on a baking tray. Drizzle over the olive oil along with a good pinch of salt, toss to mix then roast in the oven for 25 minutes.

Mix together the rice vinegar, sugar, red chilli, onion and cucumber in a small bowl and leave to steep, giving it a mix every now and then.

Coat the cod fillets in the curry paste then place onto a baking tray lined with parchment and roast in the oven for 15 minutes, by which time they should be just cooked through. When the fish has only 5 minutes to go, cut the buns in half and place in the oven to toast.

To build the burger, spread a little yoghurt onto two bun halves, load up with sliced tomato, lay the fish on top then scatter the cucumber mix over (drain off the excess vinegar). Finish with the coriander and squash the remaining bun halves on top. Serve with the sweet potato fries.

*Feel free to use any type of white fish or even chicken breast instead of the cod fillets.

Prawn & chorizo skewers

WITH MELON & BASIL

* Serves 4
* Barbecue

4 raw chorizo sausages (225g)
20 large raw prawns, peeled and cleaned
1 sweet charentais melon, peeled and cut into 3cm chunks (900g)
2 avocados, de-stoned and cut into wedges
small bunch of basil, roughly chopped
dash of red wine vinegar
dash of olive oil
salt and black pepper
50g pumpkin seeds

Fire up the barbecue, if using.

Take four large bamboo skewers and leave them to soak in water for 5 minutes.

Cut the chorizo sausages into slices about the thickness of two one-pound coins – you need to end up with 20 slices of chorizo.

To make the skewers, pierce the sharp end through the very tip of a prawn tail, then follow with a slice of chorizo. Curl the prawn around the chorizo and fix firmly by piercing through the top of the prawn. Gently slide the prawn-wrapped chorizo to the base of the skewer and repeat the process four more times, so you end up with five prawns and five thick slices of chorizo on a skewer. Repeat the process with the remaining prawns, chorizo and skewers.

To cook the skewers, lay them on the barbecue or on a large pre-heated griddle pan. Cook for about 4 minutes each side, giving them a press with the back of a spatula as they griddle to ensure even cooking.

While the skewers are cooking, gently mix together all of the remaining ingredients apart from the pumpkin seeds. Season with a tiny pinch of salt and pepper, then divide over four plates. Top each pile of melon salad with a skewer and the pumpkin seeds.

If you're cooking on the griddle you may not have a pan large enough to fit the skewers in, but you could cook in batches or grill the skewers for 4 minutes on each side.

Crab-o-cado Caprese

* Serves 4

2 ripe avocados, de-stoned
juice of 2–3 limes
1½ tbsp olive oil
salt
300g cooked white crabmeat
or prawns
2 red chillies, de-seeded and
finely chopped
bunch of chives, finely chopped
2 large tomatoes (like beef)
2 balls of mozzarella, drained
small bunch of basil, leaves only
30g toasted pine nuts

Scoop the avocado flesh into a bowl and add the lime juice and olive oil along with a good pinch of salt. Using the back of a fork, crush the avocado together with the juice and oil until you have a coarse mix.

Add the crabmeat, chillies and chives and fold them into the crushed avocado.

Slice the tomatoes thinly and divide over four plates. Sprinkle a little salt over the tomato slices. Divide the crab-o-cado over the four plates, then rip up the mozzarella and add that to the plates, too.

Finish with a scattering of basil leaves and pine nuts.

Aubergine korma
WITH SPICED MONKFISH

* Serves 2
* Make ahead
* Freeze ahead

2 tbsp coconut oil

2 onions, peeled and roughly chopped

5 cardamom pods, lightly crushed

1 tsp ground turmeric

1 tsp ground cumin

salt

1 tbsp olive oil

4 × 200g monkfish, cod or pollock fillets

4 cloves garlic, finely chopped

1 green chilli, split lengthways

1 aubergine, trimmed and cut into 2cm cubes

½ tsp ground cinnamon

400ml coconut milk

200ml chicken or veg stock (add 100ml to 'make it veg', see box)

20g ground almonds

To serve

a dollop of yoghurt

1 chilli, de-seeded and sliced

1 tbsp coriander, chopped

Preheat the oven to 210°C (fan 190°C/gas mark 6–7). Line a baking tray with baking parchment.

Melt the coconut oil in a large frying pan over a medium to high heat. Blitz the onions to a smooth puree and then tip into the hot coconut oil along with the cardamom pods. Fry, stirring regularly for 10 minutes, by which time the onions will be meltingly soft and lightly coloured.

While the onions are cooking, sprinkle half of the turmeric and cumin into a large dish along with half a teaspoon of salt and the olive oil. Give the ingredients a good mix to combine, then swish the fish in the mixture until well coated and roast in the oven for 15 minutes.

Add the garlic, green chilli and aubergine to the pan with the onions and stir-fry for 1 minute. Sprinkle in the remaining turmeric and cumin with all the cinnamon and continue to stir-fry for 30 seconds before adding the coconut milk and stock. Bring the whole lot to a simmer and cook for 10–12 minutes, or until the aubergine is just tender.

When the aubergine is tender, stir in the ground almonds.

Serve the aubergine korma topped with the monkfish, a dollop of yoghurt, sliced chilli and a generous sprinkling of chopped coriander.

> **MAKE IT VEG**
> Add a handful of cauliflower florets, trimmed green beans and 2 chopped tomatoes in with the aubergine. Top with toasted pumpkin seeds.

Roast salmon

WITH CHORIZO & ALMONDS

* Serves 4

1 tbsp coconut oil

225g raw chorizo, cut into
3cm pieces

2 red onions, peeled and cut into
thin wedges

2 red peppers, de-seeded and
cut into strips

1 courgette, trimmed and cut
into half-moons

4 × 175g salmon fillets, skin on

50g kale, thick stalks removed

80g blanched almonds

1 lemon, cut into wedges,
to serve

Preheat the oven to 200°C (fan 180°C/gas mark 6). Dollop
the coconut oil onto a large roasting tray and slide the tray
into the oven to warm up for 5 minutes.

Remove the tray from the oven and carefully lay on it the chorizo,
red onions, peppers and courgette, then roast all together in the
oven for 15 minutes.

Remove the tray from the oven, give all the ingredients a bit of a
turn and lay the salmon on top, skin-side up. Scatter on the kale
and then finally the blanched almonds, and bake in the oven for
a final 10 minutes.

Serve up over four plates along with a good wedge of lemon.

Smoked haddock

BAKED ORZO

* Serves 4

1 tbsp coconut oil

2 cloves garlic, finely chopped

2cm ginger, peeled and finely chopped

1 leek, trimmed, washed and finely sliced

1 onion, peeled and diced

200g smoked haddock, skinned and cut into 2cm chunks

250g orzo

1½ tsp curry powder

300ml skimmed milk

200ml fish stock

90g frozen peas

6 eggs

small bunch of chives, to serve

Preheat the oven to 190°C (fan 170°C/gas mark 5).

Melt the coconut oil in a large flameproof casserole dish over a medium to high heat, then add the garlic, ginger, leek and onion and cook, stirring regularly, for 6–7 minutes to soften all the vegetables.

Add the smoked haddock, orzo and curry powder and stir to combine with all the other ingredients.

Pour in the milk, fish stock and peas. Bring up to a simmer, clamp on a lid and slide the dish into the oven. Bake for 10 minutes, then carefully remove it and take off the lid. Use a spoon to make a small hole in the cooking pasta and then crack an egg in. Repeat the process a further five times, then quickly replace the lid and bake for 5 minutes.

Serve up the orzo topped with chopped chives.

Thai cod
IN A BAG

* Serves 4

300ml coconut water
1 fish stock cube
2 lemongrass stalks, bruised with the side of a knife
4 cloves garlic, bashed with your palm
2 bird's eye chillies, split open lengthways
2 kaffir lime leaves
5 spring onions, trimmed and finely sliced
2 tbsp fish sauce
800g skinless cod loin
125g baby sweetcorn, cut in half lengthways
150g midget trees (tenderstem broccoli), thick stalks cut in half lengthways

To serve
small bunch of coriander
small bunch of basil
500g pre-cooked rice

Preheat the oven to 200°C (fan 180°C/gas mark 6).

Heat the coconut water in a saucepan over a low heat. When warm, dissolve the fish stock cube in the coconut water, then add the lemongrass, garlic, chillies, lime leaves and three of the sliced spring onions. Let the ingredients simmer for 3 minutes, then turn off the heat and add the fish sauce.

Roll out a piece of kitchen foil, big enough to cover a large, flat baking tray. Cut off a slightly smaller piece of baking parchment and place in the middle of the foil. Lay the fish in the middle of the paper, then scatter with the sweetcorn and midget trees.

Draw the sides of the foil up a bit around the cod, then carefully pour over the perfumed fish stock, making sure not to lose any over the sides. Finally draw up the foil over the fish to create a large 'tent-like' structure over the ingredients.

Bake the fish in the oven for 15 minutes, then remove and leave to sit for 5 minutes before carefully cutting open (beware the sudden escape of steam when you first cut into the foil).

Sprinkle with the chopped coriander and basil and serve up the fish and sauce on top of steaming rice.

* I like using pre-cooked rice, but if you prefer you could cook 170g rice according to packet instructions.

Salmon ceviche

* Serves 2

250g fresh best-quality sushi-grade skinless salmon

2 tbsp white wine vinegar

1 tsp dijon mustard

25ml olive oil

2 eggs

1 avocado, de-stoned and cut into thin wedges

6 cherry tomatoes, cut in half

2 small handfuls of watercress

Carefully slice the salmon into eight roughly equal slices, cutting along the length of the flesh. The slices should be about 5mm thick.

Put a pan of water on to boil.

Lay the slices in the centre of two clean plates, then spoon over 1½ tablespoons of the white wine vinegar. Leave the salmon to sit in the vinegar for 15 minutes.

Whisk together the remaining vinegar with the dijon mustard and olive oil, and leave to one side.

Gently lower your eggs into the boiling water and cook for 8 minutes, then immediately drain the hot water and pour over cold water straight from the tap. This not only helps stop the eggs from overcooking, but also makes them easier to peel. Peel the eggs and slice.

When your salmon has had its time in the vinegar, start building your salad by layering up the avocado, cherry tomatoes, egg and avocado slices, then finally a pile of watercress and a drizzle of the dressing.

Grilled mackerel
WITH BEETROOT & POMEGRANATE SLAW

* Serves 2
* Barbecue

2 large mackerel fillets
salt
¼ red cabbage, cored and finely shredded (140g)
2 small cooked beetroot, drained and diced (150g)
30g pomegranate seeds
2 spring onions, sliced
40g mayonnaise
½ small bunch of dill, chopped
40g walnuts, roughly chopped

Fire up the barbecue or preheat your grill to high.

To barbecue the fish without it flaking off, drizzle a little oil on an old, flat baking tray, salt the skin-side of the mackerel then lay on the tray, skin-side up. Put the tray straight onto the hot barbecue then close the lid and cook for anywhere between 5 and 10 minutes, depending on the heat of your barbecue. Don't turn the fish.

If you're grilling in the oven, lay the mackerel fillets on the grill tray skin-side up and sprinkle generously with salt. Slide the fillets under the grill and cook without turning for 6–7 minutes – the skin should blister and darken in places, but also crisp up. The flesh will be perfectly cooked through. Shut the grill door and turn the heat off.

Mix together all of the remaining ingredients, apart from the walnut pieces, to create a dark purple coleslaw. Serve up, topped with the mackerel fillets and a scattering of walnut pieces.

* You can make the slaw ahead – it may bleed a little, but it will still taste great.

Soba noodles
WITH TUNA & CUCUMBER

* Serves 2

200g soba noodles
2 pak choy, cut into quarters lengthways
6cm ginger, peeled
1½ tbsp light soy sauce
1½ tbsp rice wine vinegar
2 tsp sesame oil
¼ cucumber, de-seeded and cut into half-moons
½ tbsp coconut oil
2 x 175g tuna steaks
2 spring onions, finely sliced

Bring a large pan of water to the boil and add the soba noodles. Cook the noodles according to the packet instructions, but when you have 2 minutes left, add the pak choy.

Drain the noodles and pak choy, then run them under cold water to cool them completely.

Grate the ginger over a clean cloth or fresh piece of kitchen roll. When all the ginger has been grated, gather up the sides of the cloth or paper and gently squeeze the flesh to extract just the juice. You are looking to extract 1½ tablespoons of juice from the flesh. Discard the wrung-out ginger when you have collected the juice.

Add the soy sauce, rice wine vinegar and sesame oil to the ginger juice and stir to mix well. Pour the dressing over the cooled noodles and add the sliced cucumber. Leave the mix to sit while you cook the tuna.

Melt the coconut oil over a high heat in a large non-stick frying pan, then gently lay the tuna steaks in the pan and fry for about 1 minute on each side. Remove the steaks to a plate.

Serve up the soba noodles topped with the tuna and a sprinkling of sliced spring onions.

Photo overleaf

You can buy soba noodles at the supermarket, but if you can get them from your local Asian store, do so – they will be better quality.

TUNA & AVO
poke bowl

* Serves 2

2 avocados, de-stoned, flesh cut
into rough 1.5cm cubes

325g fresh good-quality sushi-
grade tuna, cut into 2cm chunks

4cm ginger, peeled and
finely chopped

juice of 2 limes

4 spring onions, trimmed and
finely sliced

2½ tsp light soy sauce

1½ tsp sesame oil

1 large baby gem lettuce,
trimmed and shredded

10 cherry tomatoes,
sliced in half

salt

black sesame seeds, to serve

Simply toss all the ingredients – apart from the sesame seeds –
together until well combined. Check for seasoning, adding a little
salt if you think it needs it.

Divide over two plates, then sprinkle with sesame seeds.

Crunchy polenta cod
WITH WHITE BEAN STEW

* Serves 4

1½ tbsp coconut oil

1 red onion, peeled and diced

100g smoked back bacon, all fat trimmed, cut into 1cm strips

1 large carrot, peeled and diced

2 sticks of celery, trimmed and diced

1 tsp fennel seeds

280g cherry tomatoes, sliced in half

400g tin of cannellini beans, drained and rinsed

½ tbsp tomato puree

200ml chicken stock

90g quick-cook polenta

8 × 80g skinless pieces of cod loin

2 big fistfuls of baby spinach leaves

Heat half of the coconut oil in a large high-sided frying pan, and then add the red onion, smoked bacon, carrot, celery and fennel seeds and fry, stirring regularly for 6–7 minutes or until the vegetables are just starting to soften.

Drop in the cherry tomatoes and fry for 2 minutes, or until they just start to lose their shape. Add the beans and the puree and stir to combine everything.

Pour in the stock and bring to the boil. Reduce to a simmer and leave to bubble away for 10 minutes, keeping half an eye on it just in case it runs a bit dry.

While the beans are simmering, tip the polenta onto a plate. Taking each piece of cod one by one, press it into the polenta, ensuring you coat both sides. Lay the crusted piece of fish on a plate and repeat the process with the rest of the fish and the polenta.

When all your pieces of fish are coated, heat up half of the remaining oil in a large non-stick frying pan over a medium to high heat, then gently lay four of the cod pieces in the pan. Fry for about 2 minutes on each side, so that the polenta turns a dark golden yellow and the fish is perfectly steamed through. Remove the cod to a plate, wipe out the frying pan and repeat the process with the remaining oil and coated fish pieces.

Just before serving, stir the spinach leaves through the bean stew, cooking it through until it wilts.

Serve up the stew topped with the crunchy pieces of fish.

Risotto verde
WITH TUNA STEAK

* Serves 2

1 chicken stock cube
1 fish stock cube
1 tbsp coconut oil
1 leek, trimmed and shredded
½ courgette (130g), cut into
1cm dice
225g arborio rice
70g frozen peas
ice cubes
2 × 200g tuna steaks
salt and black pepper
100g watercress
sliced zest of 1 lemon, to serve

Drop the stock cubes into a jug and, using boiling water, make up 900ml of stock.

Melt half of the coconut oil in a large saucepan over a medium to high heat, then add the shredded leek and soften for 3–4 minutes. Add the courgette and rice together and continue to fry for a further 2 minutes.

For the next 20 minutes, add a ladleful of the stock at a time to the rice, while constantly stirring. Don't add too much stock to the pan otherwise you will lower the heat, which increases the cooking time. After 20 minutes you should have incorporated most of the stock into the pan, the rice should be just about cooked and your forearm should be nice and tired. Stir through the frozen peas and turn off the heat.

You're almost there.

Melt the remaining oil in a large frying pan, put a medium saucepan of water on to boil and prepare a large bowl of iced water ready for the watercress.

Season the tuna steaks on both sides with salt and pepper, then fry over a very high heat for 45 seconds on each side before removing them to a plate to rest.

Risotto verde

WITH TUNA STEAK

(continued)

When the water has come to the boil, drop in the watercress (stalks and all) and simmer for 20 seconds before draining and immediately dunking into the ice-cold water. Let the watercress cool for 20 seconds, then drain, squeezing it in your hands to remove as much liquid as possible. Drop the watercress into a blender, add 100ml of stock and blitz until smooth.

Pour any of the remaining stock into the risotto and turn the heat back on, stirring the stock in. The risotto is ready when the rice softens, but still retains a bite. Scrape the watercress puree into the rice pan and stir to turn the whole lot a vibrant green.

Serve up the risotto on a plate topped with the tuna steaks. Sprinkle over the lemon zest and enjoy the results of your hard work.

You can make and freeze the risotto ahead if you like, then defrost, warm in the microwave, and serve with freshly cooked tuna steaks.

Aubergine caponata

WITH GRILLED MACKEREL

* Serves 2
* Make ahead

1 tbsp coconut oil

2 jarred anchovies, drained and finely chopped

1 red onion, peeled and diced

1 sprig of rosemary

2 cloves garlic, diced

250g aubergine, diced

10g tomato puree

40ml balsamic vinegar

250–350ml water

35g raisins

2 mackerel, fillets only

15g pine nuts, to serve

Melt the coconut oil in a shallow saucepan over a medium to high heat. When it is melted and hot, add the anchovies, red onion, rosemary and garlic and fry, stirring regularly, for 3 minutes.

Add the aubergine pieces and continue to stir and fry for 5 minutes.

Squeeze in the tomato puree and stir to combine. 'Cook out' the tomato puree for 1 minute – it should turn a slightly darker shade of red. Pour in the balsamic and let it bubble down to almost nothing. Pour in 250ml of water and bring to the boil. Reduce to a simmer and cook the aubergine like this for 20 minutes, or until nice and soft. Add more water to the pan if it seems it is running dry. Ultimately you're after a thick mix with most of the water being evaporated, so don't go mad pouring loads in. Stir through the raisins.

While the aubergine is cooking, heat your grill to its highest setting. Slash the mackerel fillets about three times on the skin side, then sprinkle with salt. Lay the fish, skin-side up, on a baking tray lined with baking parchment, then grill for 8 minutes without turning.

The skin on the fish should become blistered and crisp, yet perfectly cooked on the flesh side. Turn off the heat and shut the grill door to keep the fish warm.

Serve up a big plate of the caponata topped with the mackerel fillets and a sprinkling of pine nuts.

Griddled tuna

WITH SWEETCORN & LETTUCE

* Serves 2
* Barbecue

2 sweetcorn cobs
1 tbsp olive oil
2 tomatoes, sliced in half
6 spring onions, trimmed and
cut into 4cm lengths
2 × 175g tuna steaks
2 baby gem lettuces, cut in half
¼ cucumber, de-seeded and cut
into 2cm chunks
juice of 2 limes
1 red chilli, de-seeded and
finely diced
salt and black pepper
25g pumpkin seeds

Fire up the barbecue, if using. Bring a large pot of water to the boil. When the water is bubbling, carefully slide in the corn cobs and boil them for 10 minutes, then drain and pat dry with a piece of kitchen roll.

Put a griddle pan on to heat, if using. Drizzle a little oil over the corn cobs and put them onto your barbecue grill or griddle pan to cook. Slick the tomatoes and onions with oil, too, and arrange them around the corn.

The corn will take up the rest of the time to cook – they seem to take an age to colour – but turn them every now and again. The spring onions will only take about 5 minutes and the tomatoes about 6 minutes. As they cook, remove them to a bowl.

When there is space, lay on the tuna steaks in the centre of the barbecue grill or griddle pan and cook for about 1 minute on each side, then remove to a plate and leave to rest.

Drizzle the baby gem halves with olive oil and lay them on the griddle to cook. While the vegetables are cooking, mix together the cucumber pieces with the lime juice and chilli and season well with salt and pepper.

When everything is cooked, shuck the corn by standing it up on your chopping board and running your knife down the kernels, which will come off in little clumps. Add the sweetcorn to the cucumber mix.

Serve up the tomatoes and baby gem on your plate, then top with the tuna and spring onions. Spoon over the cucumber and sweetcorn relish and finish with a scattering of pumpkin seeds.

This recipe is also great with chicken or turkey steak.

Crispy sole goujons
WITH BEETROOT & APPLE

* Serves 2
* Make ahead
* Freeze ahead

50g quick-cook polenta
2 sole fillets, skinned
salt
1–2 tbsp coconut oil
4 pitta breads
1 eating apple, cheeks cut off
and sliced thinly
1 baby gem lettuce, shredded
½ red onion, finely diced
1 large, cooked beetroot, diced
(100g)
40g fat-free Greek yoghurt
1 gherkin, drained and
finely diced

Tip the polenta onto a plate. Take each sole fillet and cut it in half to make eight long, thin fillets. Season the fish all over with salt and then, one at a time, press the flesh into the polenta until the fish is well coated all over.

It is likely you'll have to cook the fish in two batches, unless you have an absolutely huge frying pan. So, in your largest non-stick frying pan, melt half of the oil over a medium to high heat, then carefully lower in four of the yellowed fillets and fry for about 2 minutes on each side. Remove to a piece of kitchen roll to blot any excess oil, then repeat the process with the remaining oil and fish.

When all the fish is cooked, put the pittas on to toast, then mix together all the remaining ingredients along with roughly ½ tablespoon of water, to loosen.

When the pittas are toasted, put them on a plate and top with the beetroot and apple salad. Place a couple of the cooked goujons on each one and serve.

Crab fu yung

* Serves 6

6 eggs
1 tbsp soy sauce
2 tsp sesame oil
½ tbsp coconut oil
4 spring onions, trimmed and finely sliced
1 fat clove garlic, finely chopped
2 pak choy, broken into leaves
200g picked white crabmeat
1 red chilli, finely sliced – remove the seeds if you don't like it hot

Beat together the eggs with the soy sauce and sesame oil and leave to one side.

Melt the coconut oil in a large non-stick frying pan over a medium to high heat, then chuck in the spring onions, garlic and pak choy and fry, tossing regularly, for 2 minutes or until the pak choy starts to wilt.

Crank up the heat to maximum and pour in the egg mix. Let it sit, bubble up and set a little. You want to try and brown the base, so leave the egg to fry for about 90 seconds, then, like an omelette, start to draw in the sides so the uncooked egg moves into the gaps.

Continue to fry and move the egg around for 2–3 minutes, or until the egg is just cooked through. Don't worry about breaking the cooked egg up. Scatter with the crabmeat, toss the mix to heat it through and serve straight up, topped with the chilli slices.

Tuna steak

WITH FRIED MUSHROOM HASH

* Serves 2

350g new potatoes, scrubbed clean and sliced in half

1 tbsp coconut oil

150g mushrooms, brushed clean and roughly cut into quarters

2 large tuna steaks

4 spring onions, trimmed and finely sliced

7 cherry tomatoes, cut in half

pinch of ground turmeric

pinch of cayenne pepper

2 handfuls of spinach leaves

MAKE IT VEG

Remove the tuna steak and replace with a couple of poached eggs

---

Bring a large pot of water to the boil. When it is bubbling, drop in the potatoes and cook until tender, about 10 minutes. Drain and strain the potatoes, shaking off as much moisture as possible.

Heat up two medium frying pans over a medium to high heat and divide the oil between the two. When the oil is hot and melted, add the mushrooms to one of the pans and the tuna steaks to the other. Fry the tuna steaks for 1 minute on each side, then remove to a plate to rest.

Cook the mushrooms, without turning them too much, for 1 minute, then add the potatoes and continue to fry without stirring for a couple of minutes – you just want to colour the vegetables a little.

Add the spring onions and the cherry tomatoes to the pan and toss all together for 1 minute. Sprinkle in the turmeric and cayenne, then finish with handfuls of spinach. Turn the heat off and let the residual heat of the pan wilt the spinach.

Divide the mix over two plates, then top each mound with a tuna steak.

Salmon filo tart

* Serves 4
* Longer recipe
* Make ahead
* Freeze ahead

4 sheets of filo pastry, cut in half
40ml olive oil
1 head of broccoli, florets only
(roughly 175g) – large florets
cut in half
750g salmon fillet, skin on
80g baby spinach leaves
½ tbsp coconut oil
2 leeks, trimmed and cut into
5mm rounds
125g crème fraiche
70g cheddar, grated
1 egg, whisked
salt and black pepper
green salad, to serve

Preheat the oven to 180°C (fan 160°C/gas mark 4) and put a large pan of water on to boil.

Taking half a filo pastry sheet at a time, brush with a little olive oil and place in a deep 20cm loose-bottomed tart tin. You are aiming to totally cover the base and sides of the tin with the pastry, so arrange the pieces to cover some of the base and sides and then to hang over a little. Repeat the process with the remaining pieces of filo pastry, overlapping and arranging them to cover the tart case as completely as possible.

When you are happy with your lined tart tin, slide it into your preheated oven and bake for 12 minutes, then remove and leave to cool a little.

Meanwhile, drop your broccoli florets into the boiling water and simmer for 4 minutes before removing with a slotted spoon and cooling under cold running water.

Place the pot of water back on the hob and slide your piece(s) of fish in. Reduce the heat all the way to its lowest setting and poach the fish gently like this for 15 minutes, then remove to a plate and leave to cool a little. Put the pot of water back onto a high heat and bring to the boil.

Put the spinach into a colander, and when the water is boiling, take it off the heat and pour over the waiting spinach.

Salmon filo tart

(continued)

Run cold water over the wilted spinach and when it's cold enough, pick the spinach up in your hands and give it a good squeeze to remove as much water as possible – this is important, otherwise you'll end up with a soggy tart base.

Melt the coconut oil in a pan over a medium to high heat, then drop in the sliced leeks and give them a stir. Put a lid on the pan, reduce the heat to medium to low and cook the leeks like this for 4 minutes, until softened. Turn the heat off and stir in the crème fraiche, letting it melt in the residual heat. Stir in the grated cheddar and egg and season with a little salt and pepper.

Spoon about one third of the leek sauce on the tart base, then scatter over the spinach, giving it one final squeeze before laying it in. Peel the skin off the salmon and roughly break the flesh into large chunks, and arrange most of these all over the other ingredients. Scatter over the broccoli florets, then pour over half of the remaining sauce. Scatter over the rest of the salmon, then finally pour over the rest of the sauce – it's a full tart.

Slide the tart into your oven and bake for a final 20 minutes. Take the tart out of the oven, leave to stand for 10 minutes, then remove from the tin and serve warm with a nice green salad.

PAPAYA & CASHEWS

chilli sea bass

* Serves 2

2 x 120g sea bass fillets
salt
1 bird's eye chilli, finely chopped
1 lemongrass stalk, tender white part only, finely chopped
1 garlic clove, crushed
juice of 2 limes
1 tbsp fish sauce
2 tsp sesame oil
1 large papaya, peeled, seeds removed, flesh cut into 2cm chunks
8 cherry tomatoes, roughly cut in half
large handful of bean sprouts
½ bunch of coriander, roughly chopped
½ bunch of mint, roughly chopped
¼ cucumber, de-seeded and cut into half-moons
90g toasted cashews, roughly chopped

Preheat your grill to maximum and lay the sea bass fillets skin-side up on your grill tray. Season the skin generously with salt, then slide the fish under the grill and cook for 4–5 minutes without turning. The skin should crisp up and brown and blister in places.

Turn off the heat, shut the grill door and leave the fish to keep warm.

Mix together all of the remaining ingredients, apart from the cashews.

Pile the salad high over two plates, top with the cooked fish and finish with the cashews.

crab & sweetcorn fritters

WITH SRIRACHA MAYO

* Serves 2
* Make ahead
* Freeze ahead

200g white crabmeat

120g sweetcorn, drained

4 spring onions, trimmed and finely sliced

2 eggs

30g plain flour

salt and black pepper

1 tbsp coconut oil

50g mayonnaise

25g sriracha

juice of ½ lime

watercress, to serve

MAKE IT VEG

Blitz 200g cauliflower in a food processor until it resembles rice. Stir it into the mixture instead of the crabmeat and serve with chopped avocado.

Mix together the crabmeat, sweetcorn, spring onions, eggs and flour, along with a good pinch of salt and pepper, until you reach a thick consistency.

Melt half of the oil in a large non-stick frying pan over a medium to high heat. When the oil is melted and hot, dollop in three large mounds, using up half of the mixture. Using the back of a spoon, spread the mix out to form rough circles. Fry the fritters for 3 minutes on each side, then remove to a piece of kitchen roll to drain off any excess fat. Repeat the process with the remaining oil and mixture.

Meanwhile, whisk together the mayo, sriracha and lime juice. Serve up the cakes with a large handful of watercress and a healthy dollop of hot mayo.

PRAWN & CHICKEN
chow mein

* Serves 2

1 tbsp coconut oil

2 eggs

10 raw king prawns, peeled and cleaned

1 x 180g skinless chicken breast, cut into 1cm strips

4 spring onions, trimmed and finely sliced

3 cloves garlic, finely chopped

2 pak choy, trimmed and leaves separated

8 midget trees (tenderstem broccoli), thick stems cut in half

65g frozen peas

250g ready-to-eat egg noodles

2 tsp light soy sauce

½ tbsp kecap manis (Indonesian sweet soy sauce)

Melt a third of the oil in a large frying pan or wok over a high heat. Quickly beat the eggs together, and when the oil is melted and very hot, pour the egg in. Let the eggs puff up and fry hard for about 90 seconds. When you feel the eggs are set, flip them over and fry for a further 90 seconds – you're after a browned omelette. When cooked, tip the egg onto a piece of kitchen roll and blot off the excess oil.

Wipe the pan clean and dollop in half the remaining oil. When melted and hot, add the prawns and stir-fry for about 2 minutes or until the prawns have turned coral pink. At this point they don't have to be fully cooked through, but just coloured. Tip the prawns out and wipe out the pan.

Add the remaining oil to the pan and let it melt. When hot and melted, slide in the chicken and stir-fry for 2 minutes. Like the prawns, the chicken doesn't have to be fully cooked at this point – the idea is more to colour the meat.

Add the spring onions, garlic, pak choy, midget trees and frozen peas and stir-fry for 2 minutes. Pour in 1 tablespoon of water and let it steam through the ingredients. Add the egg noodles and stir-fry with the rest of the ingredients for 1 minute, then add the prawns back to the pan along with a second tablespoon of water. Fry the whole lot together for a minute, or until you are happy everything is fully cooked through.

Slice up the omelette into thin strips and add to the noodles. Finally, take the pan from the heat and stir through the soy sauce and kecap manis. Serve.

Cod with romesco sauce

& NEW POTATOES

* Serves 4

6 ripe tomatoes, roughly chopped

1 red onion, peeled and roughly chopped into chunks

1 red pepper, de-seeded and roughly chopped

2 red chillies, stems removed and the chillies cut in half lengthways

5 cloves garlic, left whole

drizzle of olive oil

2 slices of crusty white bread, roughly torn

800g new potatoes

½ tbsp coconut oil

4 × 200g skin-on cod fillets

salt

3 tbsp red wine vinegar

pinch of smoked paprika

basil leaves, to serve

Preheat the oven to 200°C (fan 180°C/gas mark 6).

Scatter the tomatoes, red onion, red pepper, chillies and garlic over a baking tray. Drizzle with a little olive oil, then slide into your oven and bake for 15 minutes.

Carefully remove the tray and chuck the torn-up bread on top. Return to the oven to roast for a further 10 minutes.

While the vegetables are roasting, bring a pan of water to the boil and cook the new potatoes for about 15 minutes or until just tender. Drain and keep to one side.

At the same time as the potatoes are boiling, melt the coconut oil in a large ovenproof frying pan over a medium to high heat. Season the skin side of the cod with salt, then gently lay the fish in the pan, skin-side down. Fry the fish without flipping for 4 minutes, then flip over and put the whole frying pan in the oven for 5 minutes, by which time the fish should be just cooked through.

When the vegetables have had their time in the oven, remove them and carefully transfer them, plus any juices in the pan, to a food processor. Add the red wine vinegar and paprika along with a good pinch of salt and pepper and blitz until almost smooth.

Serve up the cod and potatoes with the sauce and a scattering of basil leaves.

Miso aubergine
WITH SEA BREAM

* Serves 2

1 large aubergine, cut in half
lengthways
2 whole sea bream, gutted and
heads removed
6cm ginger, peeled and cut into
thin matchsticks
2 cloves garlic, cut thinly
3 spring onions, trimmed
and sliced
1 red chilli, de-seeded and sliced
2 tbsp light soy sauce
40g white miso
1 tsp sesame oil
3 tsp rice wine vinegar

Preheat the oven to 210°C (fan 190°C/gas mark 6–7).

Using a sharp knife, score the flesh of each aubergine half diagonally one way at roughly 2cm intervals, making sure not to cut all the way through. Score the other way to create a diamond pattern. Place both halves in a shallow bowl and pour on enough boiling water to come up the bowl about 1cm. Cover with cling film and zap in the microwave for 5 minutes.

Meanwhile, take each fish and cut three slashes into each side. Lay a large piece of kitchen foil over a baking tray, then lay a piece of baking parchment on top. Arrange the fish in the centre of the parchment. Sprinkle with the ginger, garlic, half of the spring onions and half of the red chilli. Drizzle over half of the soy sauce, then draw the foil over the fish to create a parcel. Slide the tray into the oven and bake for 15 minutes.

When the aubergine has had its time in the microwave, carefully take it out and remove the cling film. Using a knife and fork, transfer the aubergine to a baking tray and leave to steam-dry.

Mix together the miso paste, sesame oil and rice wine vinegar, along with a splash of water. Spoon the mix over the aubergine halves, then slide them into the oven for 10 minutes.

Remove the aubergine and fish from the oven and leave to sit for a couple of minutes. Being careful of steam, pull the tin foil parcel open. Drizzle with the remaining soy sauce, then scatter over the rest of the spring onions and red chilli.

Plate up with the aubergine, spooning over some of the delicious juice from the baking tray.

Spice-roasted salmon

WITH PANEER & CAULIFLOWER

* Serves 2

½ tbsp coconut oil

1 small head of cauliflower broken into small florets (360g)

½ courgette, cut into half-moons (about 130g)

1 small red onion, peeled and cut into thin wedges

1½ tsp curry powder

salt and black pepper

50g kale, thick stalks removed

125g paneer, cut into 2cm cubes

1 green chilli, cut into thin rounds

2 × 200g salmon fillets, skin on

small bunch of coriander, roughly chopped

2 tbsp Greek yoghurt

1 lemon, cut into wedges, to serve

Preheat the oven to 200°C (fan 180°C/gas mark 6). Dollop the coconut oil onto a baking tray and slide into the oven to preheat for 5 minutes.

Toss the cauliflower, courgette and red onion in a bowl with 1 teaspoon of the curry powder and a little salt and pepper. Carefully remove the hot tray from the oven and transfer the spiced vegetables onto the tray and slide back into the oven to roast for 10 minutes.

While the vegetables are roasting, toss the kale, paneer and green chilli with the remaining curry powder and another pinch of salt and pepper. Season the salmon on its skin side.

Take the tray from the oven and give the cauliflower and other vegetables a turn. Scatter them with the spiced paneer, kale and chilli, then lay the seasoned salmon fillets on top, salt-side up.

Slide the tray back into the oven and cook for a final 15 minutes.

Remove the tray and sprinkle with chopped coriander. Add a dollop of yoghurt and a wedge of lemon and serve up.

Pork

GRIDDLED
peach & asparagus
WITH BURRATA

* Serves 2
* Barbecue

1½ tbsp olive oil
2 peaches, stoned and cut
into quarters
100g asparagus
2 burrata, drained
4 slices of parma ham
2 handfuls of rocket
20g toasted, flaked almonds
a little drizzle of balsamic
vinegar

Fire up the barbecue or heat a large griddle pan over a
high heat.

Drizzle a little of the olive oil all over the peaches and asparagus
and give them a good smoosh around, so they are covered all
over with the oil.

Place the peaches and asparagus on the outer, slightly cooler
edges of the barbecue and cook for about 5 minutes. Turn the
asparagus regularly. If the peaches are ripe, they will need less
time. You are looking just to caramelize the peach flesh and to
take any hard bite away – there is no hard and fast rule to this.
Barbecue the asparagus until lightly charred and just tender.

If you are cooking on the griddle pan, cook the peaches first,
then remove the pieces to a plate and cook the asparagus for
about 4 minutes, turning regularly until lightly charred.

Lay the burrata and parma ham on a plate and then build up
the salad using the rocket, griddled peaches and asparagus,
and finish with a scattering of toasted almonds and a drizzle of
balsamic vinegar.

Photo on previous page

Manchego saltimbocca

WITH PEAR & ROCKET SALAD

* Serves 4
* Freeze ahead

4 × 175g thin pork escalopes
(roughly 18 × 12cm in size)

24 sage leaves, finely chopped

8 slices of manchego cheese,
plus a little extra for the salad,
rind removed

16 slices of parma ham

1 tbsp coconut oil

1 pear, sliced thinly

4 handfuls of rocket

40g pecan nuts,
roughly chopped

drizzle of balsamic vinegar

Take each piece of pork in turn and cut it in half widthways. Sprinkle chopped sage over both sides of the meat, then crumble a small slice of manchego onto one side of the meat.

Draw the meat over the cheese to envelop it, then wrap the small parcel in two slices of parma ham. Repeat the process with all of the remaining slices of pork and cheese until you are left with eight little wrapped parcels.

Melt half of the oil in a large non-stick frying pan over a medium to high heat, then fry four of the parcels for about 3 minutes on each side. Remove and keep warm while you repeat the process with the remaining parcels.

When you have cooked all of your saltimbocca, make a salad by tossing together the thinly sliced pear with the rocket and then shaving off fine slices of cheese with a potato peeler.

Plate up the perfect parcels with a big handful of salad, a sprinkling of chopped pecan nuts and a drizzle of balsamic.

Grilled pork chops
WITH APPLE & DILL COLESLAW

* Serves 4
* Barbecue

4 large pork chops, fat removed if you prefer

1 carrot, peeled and julienned (140g)

1 large apple, julienned (100g)

3 sticks of celery, trimmed and finely sliced on the angle (100g)

1 red onion, peeled and finely sliced

¼ small white cabbage (200g)

85g mayonnaise

1 tbsp white wine vinegar

small bunch of dill, finely chopped

2 tsp dijon mustard

watercress, to serve

Fire up the barbecue or preheat your grill to maximum.

Lay your chops on the barbecue or grill tray (if possible, cover the barbecue to ensure even cooking). Cook for 6–7 minutes, then turn the chops over and cook for a further 6–7 minutes, or until you are happy the meat is cooked through – you can check this by cutting into a thick part of the meat and ensuring the flesh has turned white.

If you're cooking under the grill, turn the heat off, shut the grill door and leave the meat to rest until you're ready to serve. Otherwise cover with foil.

While the chops are cooking, toss together the carrot, apple, celery, red onion and cabbage. Add the mayo, vinegar, dill and mustard and mix the whole lot together until the vegetables are evenly coated in the mayo mix.

Serve up the chops with a good heap of coleslaw and a handful of watercress.

Take the meat out of the fridge 15 minutes before cooking it – it ensures you can cook the meat all the way through without it drying out.

Summer salad
WITH COURGETTE & HAM

* Serves 2

3 eggs
75g gherkins, drained and
finely chopped
30g capers, drained and
roughly chopped
40ml olive oil
small bunch of dill,
finely chopped
small bunch of chives,
finely chopped
1 medium courgette
75g fresh peas
300g thick-cut, deli-style ham
30g walnuts, roughly chopped

Cook the eggs in a pan of boiling water for 8 minutes, then drain and cool under cold running water. Peel and leave to one side.

Mix together the gherkins, capers, olive oil, dill and chives in a large bowl.

Take your courgette and, using a peeler, create long thin ribbons along the entire length of the courgette. When you get close to the core, rotate the courgette and continue on the other side. You won't be able to make ribbons with the whole courgette, so just keep what's left of the core for another recipe, such as a stir-fry.

Add the courgette ribbons to the bowl of dressing along with the peas and toss the whole lot together.

Slice the boiled eggs into rounds. Build up your courgette salad on two plates, tearing the ham into it and laying on the egg slices. Finish with some chopped walnuts and get stuck in.

MAKE IT VEG
Omit the ham and replace with 1 chopped avocado and a generous sprinkling of flaxseeds.

PORK & KIDNEY BEAN
burritos

* Serves 4

600g pork tenderloin, trimmed of visible fat

1½ tsp sweet smoked paprika

½ tsp cayenne pepper – add more or less, depending on your resilience

1½ tsp ground cumin

1 red onion, finely sliced

4 cloves garlic, minced

large bunch of coriander

salt and black pepper

½ tbsp coconut oil

1 x 400g tin of chopped tomatoes

180g kidney beans (drained weight)

200g pre-cooked rice

4 large tortilla wraps

1 iceberg lettuce, shredded, to serve

Cut the pork into large 4cm chunks, then put them in a bowl and add the paprika, cayenne, cumin, onion, garlic and the finely chopped stalks of the coriander. Add a pinch of salt and pepper and give the whole lot a good stir and leave to sit for 5 minutes.

After 5 minutes, melt the coconut oil in a large frying pan over a high heat, and when the oil is hot and melted, tip the entire contents of the bowl into the pan. Fry the mix for about 5 minutes, but only stirring occasionally – you're after a bit of colour on the pork and onions if possible.

When everything in the pan is a little wilted down, pour in the chopped tomatoes and kidney beans along with a little splash of water. Bring the whole lot to the boil, then simmer for 5 minutes or until you are happy the pork is fully cooked through – you can check this by cutting into a thick piece and ensuring it has turned from fleshy pink to cooked white.

Chop up the remaining coriander leaves and stir through. Heat up the tortilla wraps – I do this in the microwave – and serve up.

Spoon some of the rice onto the wraps, add the pork and beans and finish with a good handful of shredded iceberg lettuce. Wrap up and serve up.

I like using pre-cooked rice, but if you prefer you could cook 70g rice according to packet instructions.

hickpea & veg stew

WITH PORK TENDERLOIN

* Serves 4

1 tbsp coconut oil
1 red onion, peeled and sliced
½ courgette, grated
1 small carrot, peeled and grated
3 cloves garlic, roughly chopped
1 red chilli, finely sliced – remove the seeds if you don't like it hot
½ tsp ground cumin
½ tsp ground coriander
¼ tsp cayenne pepper
salt and black pepper
300g fresh tomatoes, roughly chopped
1 × 400g tin of chickpeas, drained
65g prunes, roughly chopped
750g piece of pork tenderloin
small bunch of coriander, roughly chopped
crusty bread, to serve

Heat half of the coconut oil in a large frying pan over a medium to high heat, then add the red onion and fry for 2 minutes, stirring regularly.

Add the courgette, carrot, garlic and chilli and crank up the heat to maximum. Fry the ingredients, stirring regularly, for about 2 minutes, by which time they should be breaking down.

Reduce the heat and sprinkle in the cumin, coriander, cayenne pepper and a good pinch of both salt and pepper.

Add the tomatoes, chickpeas and prunes, along with a splash of water. As the tomatoes cook, they will break down and release liquid. However, if you feel the pan is cooking dry, then add a small splash of water. Leave the mix to cook for 10 minutes.

In the meantime, take the pork tenderloin and cut into four roughly equal cylinders, trimming off any large pieces of fat and sinew. Take each loin cylinder and slice down the length, making sure you don't cut all the way through the meat. Open the meat like a book and give it a couple of pushes with the palm of your hand. Repeat the process with the remaining pieces of meat and then season well with salt and pepper.

Melt the remaining oil in a large frying pan over a medium to high heat. When the oil is melted and hot, lay the pork tenderloins in and cook for 10 minutes, turning regularly. Remove the pork to a plate and leave to rest for 5 minutes.

Serve up the stew, slice up the tenderloin and lay it on top. Finish with coriander and wolf down with a thick slice of bread.

Harissa pork chops
WITH FENNEL & PARSLEY SALAD

* Serves 2
* Barbecue

2 large pork chops
1 heaped tablespoon of rose harissa paste
salt
8 pitted green olives, cut in half
20g preserved lemon, roughly cut into small pieces
30g walnuts, roughly chopped
40g feta, roughly crumbled
1 large fennel bulb, trimmed and finely sliced
small bunch of parsley, roughly chopped
25ml olive oil

Fire up the barbecue or turn your grill on to maximum.

Lay your pork chops on a plate and spoon on the harissa paste. Using your hands or a spoon, smother the meat with the red paste. Give them a little sprinkle of salt.

Lay your chops on the barbecue or grill tray (if possible, cover the barbecue to ensure even cooking). Cook for 6–7 minutes, then turn the chops over and cook for a further 6–7 minutes, or until you are happy the meat is cooked through – you can check this by cutting into a thick part of the meat and ensuring the flesh has turned white.

If you're cooking under the grill, turn the heat off, shut the grill door and leave the meat to rest until you're ready to serve. Otherwise cover with foil.

While the chops are cooking, place all of the remaining ingredients into a bowl and toss together.

Serve up the salad topped with a spicy pork chop.

* If you don't like pork chops, try this with lamb chops or chicken thighs.

Sausage & mushroom pie

* Serves 4
* Longer recipe
* Freeze ahead

½ tbsp coconut oil

12 sausages

2 large onions, peeled and finely sliced

2 carrots, peeled and diced

2 sticks of celery, trimmed and diced

5 sprigs of thyme

1 bay leaf

250g chestnut mushrooms, brushed clean and roughly chopped into quarters

salt and black pepper

200ml chicken stock

200ml ale (I use London Pride)

30ml Worcestershire sauce

10g cornflour

3 large sheets of filo pastry

1 tbsp olive oil

2 tsp nigella seeds

buttered greens, to serve

Melt the oil in a large, high-sided frying pan over a medium to high heat, then roll the sausages into the pan and brown all over. Don't worry about cooking the sausages through at this point – all you want is for them to go dark brown. Remove the sausages from the pan and then add the onions.

Cook the onions for about 8 minutes, or until softened and caramelized. Add the carrots, celery, thyme and bay leaf and cook for a further 2 minutes, stirring frequently over a high heat.

Add the chestnut mushrooms along with a good pinch of both salt and pepper, and continue to stir-fry for another couple of minutes, then add the stock, ale and Worcestershire sauce. Bring the liquid slowly up to the boil (rapid boiling makes it taste bitter), then reduce to a simmer and cook for 10 minutes.

Mix the cornflour with just enough water to make it into a liquid, then pour into the mix and stir to thicken.

Tip the mix into a 29 x 20cm baking dish and preheat the oven to 190°C (fan 170°C/gas mark 5). Let the mix cool just a little in the baking dish, then take the sheets of filo, scrunch a little and cover the filling. Brush randomly with olive oil and sprinkle with the nigella seeds.

Slide the dish into the oven and bake for 20–25 minutes, by which time the pastry will be crisp and coloured on top and cooked through underneath. Serve up with steaming buttered greens.

ROAST CHICORY AND PECANS
with salami

* Serves 2

4 chicory heads – I like to use
2 red and 2 yellow
2 tbsp olive oil
½ red onion, peeled and
finely sliced
juice of ½ orange
½ tbsp red wine vinegar
½ fennel bulb, trimmed and
finely sliced
16 slices of best-quality salami
30g pecans, roughly chopped

Preheat the oven to 190°C (fan 170°C/gas mark 5).

Cut the chicory heads in half lengthways, discarding any
of the brown outer leaves. Lay the chicory on a roasting
tray, cut-side up, and drizzle with a little olive oil. Roast in
the oven for 25 minutes until lightly caramelized and tender,
but still holding their shape.

Meanwhile, drop the sliced red onion into a bowl and pour
over the orange juice and red wine vinegar. Leave the onions
to macerate while the chicory heads are cooking.

When the chicory heads have had their time in the oven, divide
them between the two plates. Spoon some of the macerated
onions over the chicory, reserving the soaking juices.

Pile up the fennel, salami and pecans and finally finish with
spoonfuls of the soaking juices.

Beef &
Lamb

KOFTA-STUFFED
Romano peppers

* Serves 4

4 large Romano peppers, halved lengthways, seeds removed

10ml olive oil

1 tbsp coconut oil

2 red onions, peeled and finely sliced

3 cloves garlic, finely chopped

1 aubergine, trimmed and diced into 1cm cubes (250g)

250g lamb mince

250g beef mince

½ tsp ground cinnamon

1 tsp ground cumin

½ tsp sweet smoked paprika

salt and black pepper

1 tbsp tomato puree

100ml beef stock

70g pine nuts

½ bunch of coriander, roughly chopped

225g pizza mozzarella, patted dry

rocket, to serve

Preheat the oven to 210°C (fan 190°C/gas mark 6–7).

Lay the peppers on a baking tray in a single layer, drizzle over the olive oil and roast in the hot oven for 20 minutes.

Meanwhile, melt the coconut oil in a large frying pan over a medium to high heat, then add the red onion and garlic and fry for 3–4 minutes or until just soft.

Crank up the heat to maximum and add the aubergine and both types of mince. Fry the ingredients over the high heat, stirring occasionally for a few minutes, breaking up the mince with a wooden spoon. Sprinkle in the cinnamon, cumin and paprika and stir to incorporate.

Season with a generous amount of salt and pepper, then add the tomato puree along with the beef stock and let the mixture simmer away – you don't want it to be too wet. After a couple of minutes, turn the heat off and stir through the pine nuts and chopped coriander.

Remove the roasted peppers from the oven. They should have collapsed a little but still be holding their shape. Carefully drain off liquid that may have been produced while roasting, then fill the cavities with the mixture. Don't worry if the mixture falls over the side.

Slice or tear the mozzarella and arrange over the top of the mince, then slide the tray back into the oven and bake for a further 10 minutes. The mozzarella will have melted nicely by this point. Serve up with a generous helping of rocket.

Spiced lamb chops
WITH CUCUMBER SALAD

* Serves 4
* Barbecue

2 tsp ground cumin
3 tsp sea salt
12 lamb loin chops
100g Greek yoghurt
bunch of dill, roughly chopped
juice of ½ lemon
½ cucumber, de-seeded and cut into chunks
12 cherry tomatoes, cut in half
½ red onion, peeled and diced
2 tbsp balsamic vinegar
salt and black pepper
60g toasted pine nuts

Fire up the barbecue or preheat your grill to maximum. Mix together the cumin and salt and season your lamb chops all over with the spiced salt.

Lay your chops on the outer, slightly cooler edges of the barbecue, or grill tray (if possible, cover the barbecue to ensure even cooking). Cook for 5–6 minutes, then turn the chops over and cook for a further 5–6 minutes, or until you are happy the meat is cooked through.

If you're cooking under the grill, turn the heat off, shut the grill door and leave the meat to rest until you're ready to serve (at least 5 minutes). Otherwise cover with foil.

Tip the yoghurt into a bowl and mix it with three-quarters of the dill and the lemon juice.

Mix together the cucumber, cherry tomatoes, red onion and balsamic vinegar, seasoning with a little salt and pepper.

Serve up the spiced lamb chops, with the salad, yoghurt and a scattering of the reserved dill and the pine nuts.

Paprika lamb kebabs

WITH WHIPPED HERB RICOTTA

* Serves 4
* Barbecue

drizzle of olive oil
½ tsp ground cumin
½ tsp sweet smoked paprika
salt and black pepper
700g lamb steak, cut into 3cm chunks, hard fat removed (if any)
350g ricotta
2 tbsp extra virgin olive oil
small bunch of chives, finely chopped
½ bunch of parsley, finely chopped
juice of ½ lemon
3 cooked beetroot, drained and cut into large chunks
4 handfuls of rocket
40g walnuts, roughly chopped

Fire up the barbecue or put a heavy-based griddle pan on to heat over a medium to high flame.

Mix together the oil, cumin and paprika along with a big pinch of salt and pepper. Thread the meat onto four long skewers – you want the meat to touch, but don't squash it on otherwise it won't cook at all.

Swoosh the skewered meat through the spice mix, trying to ensure a thin, even layer all over. Lay the kebabs on the outer, slightly cooler part of the barbecue, or the hot griddle pan and fry, turning every 2–3 minutes for about 10 minutes, or until the meat is lovely and browned on the outside and just cooked through on the inside. Remove the meat to rest for at least 5 minutes.

While the meat is resting, tip the ricotta into a bowl and add the extra virgin olive oil along with a good pinch of salt. Whip the ricotta with a whisk for about 30 seconds or until it is totally smooth. Stir through the chopped chives, parsley and lemon juice and then divide over four plates. Place a lamb skewer onto each plate, then divide out the beetroot, rocket and walnuts.

AVOCADO & GOAT'S CHEESE WITH
grilled lamb chops

* Serves 2

6 lamb loin chops
salt and black pepper
10 cherry tomatoes
1 large avocado, de-stoned
70g soft goat's cheese
60g Greek yoghurt
30ml olive oil
small bunch of chives,
finely sliced
½ small bunch of mint,
finely chopped
rocket, to serve

Turn on your grill to maximum. Lay the lamb chops on your grill tray and season with a little salt and pepper. Cook the chops under the grill for 8 minutes, then flip them, scatter the cherry tomatoes on the same tray and cook for a further 4–5 minutes. Shut the grill door, turn off the heat and leave the chops to rest.

While the lamb is resting, place the avocado flesh, goat's cheese, yoghurt and olive oil into a food processor and blitz until smooth. Remove to a bowl and stir in the chives and mint along with a little salt and pepper.

Serve up the chops with a big dollop of the avocado tzatziki, the cherry tomatoes and a big handful of rocket.

Quick spiced beef

* Serves 4

½ tbsp coconut oil
1 red onion, peeled and diced
1 aubergine, trimmed and cut into 1cm dice
1 red pepper, de-seeded and cut into 1cm dice
3 cloves garlic, finely chopped
600g beef mince
½ tsp ground cinnamon
½ tsp ground cumin
1 tbsp flour
200ml beef stock
40g raisins

To serve

500g pre-cooked rice
shredded lettuce
small bunch of coriander, roughly chopped

Melt the coconut oil in a large frying pan over a medium to high heat, then add the red onion and cook for 2 minutes. Chuck in the aubergine, red pepper and chopped garlic. Fry the ingredients for 5 minutes.

Crank up the heat to maximum and push the vegetables to one side. Plonk the meat straight into the frying pan and fry without moving it for 1 minute, then get stuck in and break the meat up. Keep frying and breaking up the meat for a couple of minutes or until it is well broken up.

Add the ground spices and flour and mix to make sure there are no lumps, then pour in the stock and add the raisins. Bring the liquid to the boil and simmer for 5 minutes.

Serve up the spiced beef on rice with a side of shredded lettuce and a sprinkling of chopped coriander.

* I like using pre-cooked rice, but if you prefer you could cook 170g rice according to packet instructions.

Grilled sirloin wraps

WITH WASABI DRESSING

* Serves 2

2 cloves garlic, minced

3cm ginger, peeled and minced

1 tbsp soy sauce

1 tbsp honey

2 sirloin steaks, visible fat removed

200g pre-cooked rice

½ tbsp wasabi

1½ tbsp rice wine vinegar

1 tsp sesame oil

2 plain tortilla wraps

4 radishes, thinly sliced

2 spring onions, trimmed and finely sliced

shredded iceberg lettuce, to serve

Mix together the garlic, ginger, soy sauce and honey until combined. Lay the steaks in the mixture, swishing them about a bit to make sure they're evenly coated, then leave the steaks to sit for 10 minutes.

Heat a griddle pan over maximum heat. When the steaks have had their 10 minutes, take them from the bowl, scraping off any excess marinade, and lay the meat gently in the griddle pan. Fry, turning regularly, for 4 minutes on each side. Remove the steaks to a plate to rest.

While the steaks are resting, ping the rice in the microwave, then whisk together the wasabi, vinegar and sesame oil. Warm through the tortillas in either the microwave or a dry frying pan.

Lay out the tortillas, then divide the rice over the middle of each one. Slice the steak, then place it on top of the rice and drizzle the wasabi dressing over the cooked meat. Pile up the radishes, spring onions and lettuce, then wrap the tortillas as well as you can and chow down.

* Make sure you cook the steaks from room temperature, otherwise you may burn them on the outside and leave them raw in the middle. I like using pre-cooked rice, but if you prefer you could cook 70g rice according to packet instructions.

SWEDISH-STYLE
meatballs

* Serves 2

450ml double cream
2 cloves garlic, minced
2 bay leaves
½ tbsp coconut oil
800g small ready-made
meatballs (or see Tip below)
20g gruyère or mature
cheddar, grated
75g pomegranate seeds –
optional

To serve
large bunch of dill, leaves only
steamed greens

Pour the cream into a wide saucepan, add the garlic and
bay leaves and bring to a low simmer, stirring frequently.
Let the cream simmer for 5 minutes to reduce by a third.

While the cream is reducing, melt half of the coconut oil in a
large frying pan over a medium to high heat. When the oil is
melted and hot, roll half of the meatballs in and brown all over.
The meatballs should be virtually cooked by the time they are
browned. Remove the balls to a plate with a slotted spoon,
wipe out the pan with some kitchen roll and repeat the process
with the remaining oil and balls.

Reduce the heat under the cream and stir in the grated cheese
until it has melted and is fully incorporated. Tip the balls, along
with any residual cooking liquids, into the cheese and gently
stir to coat. Serve up the meatballs scattered with pomegranate
seeds, if using, and dill, alongside some steamed greens.

** To make your own meatballs, mix together 750g beef mince,
35g fresh breadcrumbs and 1 egg in a bowl using your
hands. Season with salt and pepper and shape into roughly
20 little balls. Continue with the recipe.*

Roast pepper gnocchi
WITH SIRLOIN STEAK

* Serves 4

1 tbsp coconut oil

1 red onion, peeled and finely sliced

small bunch of basil (20g), roughly chopped

100g jarred red pepper, drained and cut into 1cm strips

2 × 200g sirloin steaks, visible fat removed

300g ready-to-cook fresh gnocchi

balsamic glaze dressing, to finish

Melt half of the oil in a large frying pan over a medium heat, and at the same time put a large saucepan of water on to boil. As soon as the oil has melted and is hot, add the onion and fry gently, stirring regularly for about 8 minutes or until the onions are very soft.

Put a second pan on over a high heat for the steaks.

Add half of the chopped basil to the onions, along with the roasted red pepper, and stir everything together. As soon as the peppers are warmed through, turn the heat off under the pan.

Add the remaining coconut oil to the pan over the high heat, then lay in the steaks. Cook the steaks according to preference – I like my steak medium rare, so 2½ minutes on each side, turning regularly – then leave to rest until you're ready to eat.

While the steak is resting, carefully drop the gnocchi into the boiling water and simmer according to packet instructions (normally about 3 minutes). You know they're done when they float to the surface.

-7

Roast pepper gnocchi

WITH SIRLOIN STEAK

(continued)

Before draining off the gnocchi, save about a quarter of a mugful of the cooking water and add to the pan with the sweated onions and peppers. Drain the gnocchi and add to the onion pan.

Turn the heat back on under the onions, which now have the gnocchi in as well, and gently stir the whole lot together until the gnocchi are nicely covered with the sauce and everything is heated through.

Stir through the remaining basil, leaving a little for garnish if you like, then serve up on two plates. Slice the steak and serve on top of the gnocchi, all finished with a tasty drizzle of balsamic glaze.

Sumac lamb chops
WITH ROAST LETTUCE

* Serves 2

1 clove garlic, grated
1½ tbsp olive oil
2 baby gem lettuces
10 cherry tomatoes
6 lamb chops
salt and black pepper
2 tsp sumac
65g Greek yoghurt
25g tahini
juice of ½ lemon
40g pomegranate seeds
½ small bunch of mint,
leaves only

Preheat the oven to 210°C (fan 190°C/gas mark 6–7) and turn your grill up to maximum.

Mix together the grated garlic and olive oil in a small bowl.

Cut the baby gem lettuces in half lengthways and lay on a roasting tray. Place the tomatoes close by, then spoon about two-thirds of the garlic and oil over the cut side of the lettuces and the tomatoes. Slide the tray into the oven and roast for 12 minutes.

Lay the lamb chops down and season with salt and pepper, then sprinkle over the sumac and rub to ensure an even coating. Cook the lamb chops under the hot grill for 7 minutes, then flip and cook for a further 4 minutes on the other side. When they are cooked, turn the heat off and shut the grill door to keep them warm until you're ready to eat.

Mix together the remaining garlic oil, yoghurt, tahini and lemon juice in a small bowl along with about 75ml of water to make a fairly runny sauce.

Plate up the roasted lettuce topped with the tomatoes and the spiced lamb chops and finish with the garlicky sauce, pomegranate seeds and mint leaves.

* You could also use the slightly cheaper lamb-leg steaks for this recipe.

Fennel & lemon lamb chops

WITH BUTTERY PEAS

* Serves 2

6 lamb loin chops
1½ tsp fennel seeds
1 lemon
salt and black pepper
300g frozen peas
30g butter
1 red chilli, de-seeded and finely chopped
3 spring onions, trimmed and finely sliced
½ bunch of mint, leaves roughly chopped
watercress, to serve

Crank up your grill to maximum and lay the lamb chops on your grill tray.

Using a pestle and mortar, smash up the fennel seeds – not to a dust, but they should become pretty small. (If you don't have a pestle and mortar, just lay the seeds on your board and chop through them a few times.) Sprinkle the fennel seeds all over the lamb chops, then grate lemon zest over them, too. Season with salt and pepper, then grill for 8 minutes before turning and grilling for a further 6 minutes. Turn off the heat, shut the grill door and leave the lamb to rest.

While the lamb is cooking, put a pot of water on to boil. When the water is bubbling away, add the peas and cook for about 6 minutes – you are looking to slightly overcook the peas. Drain the peas and leave to one side.

Add the butter to the still-warm saucepan and melt over a medium heat. Chuck in the red chilli and spring onions and fry for 2 minutes. Tumble the peas back in and give the whole lot a good toss.

Turn the heat off under the peas and use a potato masher to rough them up – you're not trying to mash them all, more just crush them.

Serve up the peas topped with the lamb chops, mint leaves, a handful of watercress and the zested lemon, wedged.

* Lamb-leg steaks are a lovely cheaper option.

Sirloin steaks

WITH GARLICKY CREAMY SPINACH

* Serves 2

20g butter
2 cloves garlic, finely chopped
450g frozen spinach
½ tbsp coconut oil
2 sirloin steaks
100ml double cream
50g parmesan
grating of nutmeg

Melt the butter in a medium frying pan over a medium to high heat, then add the chopped garlic and fry for 1 minute. Add the frozen spinach to the pan and reduce the heat to medium. For the next 5 minutes, warm the spinach through in the pan, giving it the occasional prod to break the large lumps up.

While the spinach is defrosting, melt the coconut oil in a second frying pan over a high heat. When the oil is hot and melted, cook the steaks according to preference – I like my steaks medium rare, so 2½ minutes on each side, turning regularly – then leave to rest until you're ready to eat.

As the spinach defrosts it will release a lot of water. Without destroying the spinach, drain off as much as you can, then stir in the double cream and bring to a light boil. Turn the heat off underneath, and stir through the parmesan and grated nutmeg.

Divide the spinach over two plates, then top with the perfectly cooked steaks.

SIRLOIN STEAK WITH
chimichurri

* Serves 2

2 tbsp olive oil

1 banana shallot, peeled and diced

1 tsp thyme leaves

3g oregano leaves, roughly chopped

7g parsley leaves, roughly chopped

150g cherry tomatoes, cut in half

salt and pepper

2 tsp balsamic vinegar

½ tbsp coconut oil

2 sirloin steaks

grilled or steamed midget trees (tenderstem broccoli), to serve

Pour the olive oil into a medium saucepan over a medium to low heat. Add the shallot, thyme, oregano, parsley and cherry tomatoes and leave to 'cook' very gently, stirring every now and then for 15 minutes, by which time all the ingredients will have released their flavours. Turn the heat off, sprinkle in a good amount of salt and pepper along with the balsamic and stir.

While the sauce is cooking, melt the coconut oil in a frying pan over a high heat. Lay in the steaks and cook according to preference – I like my steak medium rare, so 2½ minutes on each side, turning regularly – then leave to rest until you're ready to eat.

Serve up the steak with a generous helping of midget trees, all topped with the tasty sauce.

Beef & lemongrass

NOODLE SOUP

* Serves 2

1 tbsp coconut oil

2 lemongrass stalks, tender white part only, finely sliced

1 stick of celery, finely chopped

1 star anise

1 stick of cinnamon

4cm ginger, peeled and roughly chopped

1 bird's eye chilli, split lengthways

juice and zest of 1 lime

4 spring onions, trimmed and finely sliced

2 tomatoes, roughly chopped

600ml chicken stock

2 sirloin steaks

300g ready-to-eat rice noodles

1 tbsp fish sauce

fresh coriander, to serve

Melt half of the coconut oil in a saucepan over a medium to high heat, then add the lemongrass, celery, star anise, cinnamon stick, ginger, chilli, lime zest and two of the sliced spring onions. Let the ingredients fry for a couple of minutes, then add the chopped-up tomatoes and fry until the tomatoes begin to break down.

Pour in the chicken stock and bring the whole lot to the boil, then reduce to a low simmer and cook for 10 minutes.

While the soup is simmering away, melt the remaining oil in a large frying pan over a high heat, then gently lay the steaks in the pan. Fry the steaks for 4 minutes on each side, turning regularly. When the steaks have had their cooking time, remove them to a plate to rest.

Bring a kettle to the boil and tip the noodles into a sieve. When the kettle has boiled, pour the water over the noodles. Give the noodles a shake to remove the excess liquid, then divide between two deep bowls.

Sieve the simmered soup broth into a jug and stir in the fish sauce and the juice of the lime. Pour the broth over the noodles, then slice up the steak and lay it on top of the noodles. Finish with a scattering of coriander and the remaining two finely sliced spring onions.

Drink up and feel yourself being restored.

Beef-stuffed aubergine

WITH HALLOUMI & GREEN OLIVES

* Serves 2

2 aubergines
drizzle of olive oil
½ tbsp coconut oil
1 red onion, peeled and diced
2 cloves garlic, finely chopped
½ tsp fenugreek seeds
½ tsp ground turmeric
½ tsp chilli powder
½ tsp ground coriander
400g beef mince
100g mushrooms, brushed
clean and roughly chopped
into small pieces
1 beef stock cube
salt and black pepper
40g pitted green olives, drained
and roughly chopped
100g halloumi, grated
rocket, to serve
drizzle of balsamic vinegar

Preheat the oven to 200°C (fan 180°C/gas mark 6).

Take each aubergine one at a time and cut in half lengthways. Score the flesh, making sure not to cut all the way through the skin. Using a spoon, scratch out the aubergine flesh, leaving only a thin flesh border attached to the skin. Lay the hulled-out aubergine halves on a baking tray, drizzle with olive oil and roast in the oven for 15 minutes.

While the aubergine is baking, melt the coconut oil in a frying pan over a medium to high heat, then add the red onion, garlic and fenugreek seeds and fry, stirring regularly, for 5 minutes.

Sprinkle in the rest of the spices and stir to combine. Crank up the heat to maximum and add the beef mince. Leave it without prodding for 2 minutes to try and brown a little. Add the mushrooms to the pan and stir together. Cut the aubergine flesh (about 200g) into small pieces, then add this to the pan, too.

Crumble the stock cube and stir in, along with a good pinch of salt and pepper. Put a lid on the pan and leave to cook for 10 minutes.

Turn off the heat, remove the lid and stir through the green olives. The aubergines will have cooked by now, so carefully remove them and then fill the cavity with the beef mixture. Sprinkle over the halloumi, then slide the halves back into the oven for a final 5–10 minutes.

Serve up with a big handful of rocket and a drizzling of balsamic.

OLIVE, ARTICHOKE, QUINOA &
steak salad

* Serves 2

½ tbsp coconut oil

2 sirloin steaks, any visible fat removed

350g pre-cooked quinoa – red and white mixed

175g jarred artichokes, thoroughly drained and roughly chopped

100g pitted green olives, drained and roughly chopped

1 preserved lemon, peel only, finely chopped

large bunch of parsley, roughly chopped

2 small handfuls of rocket, to serve

Melt the coconut oil in a large frying pan over a high heat, then gently lay the steaks in it and fry for 4 minutes on each side, turning regularly. Remove the steaks to a plate to rest.

Zap the quinoa in a microwave according to the packet instructions. When hot, carefully tip into a large bowl and add the artichokes, olives, preserved lemon peel and parsley. Give the whole lot a good stir and then divide over two plates.

Slice the steak into thick chunks and top the quinoa with it. Finish with a little handful of rocket.

STEAK WITH KALE, TAHINI &
sesame greens

* Serves 2

1 tbsp coconut oil

2 cloves garlic, finely chopped

200g kale, thick stalks removed

½ courgette, trimmed and cut into half-moons

125g midget trees (tenderstem broccoli), thick stalks cut in half lengthways

150ml hot chicken stock

2 sirloin steaks

salt

30g tahini

3 tsp sesame oil

2 red chillies, de-seeded and finely chopped

sesame seeds, to serve

Melt half of the coconut oil in a large frying pan over a medium to high heat, then add the chopped garlic and cook for 30 seconds. Add the kale, courgette and midget trees and fry, stirring regularly, for 3 minutes.

Pour the hot stock into the pan with the greens. Reduce the heat to medium and cook for 5 minutes, stirring every now and again.

In the meantime, heat the remaining oil in a frying pan over a high heat, and gently lay in the steaks. Cook the steaks for 4 minutes on each side, turning them regularly as they cook. Remove the steaks to a plate to rest and season them with salt.

Check the vegetables are just tender, then take the pan off the heat. Mix the tahini with the sesame oil in a small bowl.

Serve up the greens topped with the sliced steak, red chilli, sesame seeds and a drizzle of the sesame and tahini dressing.

One-pan steak
WITH DEVILLED MUSHROOMS

* Serves 2

¾ tbsp coconut oil

1 red onion, peeled and diced

8 chestnut mushrooms, brushed clean and roughly cut in half

3 sprigs of thyme

350g fillet steak, cut into 3cm chunks

¾ tsp sweet smoked paprika

pinch of cayenne pepper

salt and black pepper

200g crème fraiche

1½ tsp dijon mustard

2 large handfuls of baby spinach leaves

juice of ½ lemon

steamed green beans, to serve

Melt half of the coconut oil in a large frying pan over a medium to high heat. then add the diced onion and fry for 3–4 minutes, stirring regularly.

Crank up the heat to maximum and toss in the chopped mushrooms and thyme sprigs. Fry the ingredients all together, stirring every now and again – the aim is to soften the vegetables, but also to catch a little colour without burning.

Transfer the onions and mushrooms to a plate. Melt the remaining coconut oil in the pan, then add the steak and fry hard, turning only now and again. You want to colour the meat – the cooking will take care of itself.

Once the meat is well coloured, mix in the mushrooms and onions, then sprinkle in the paprika and cayenne along with a good pinch of salt and pepper.

Reduce the heat to low and stir in the crème fraiche. Let the crème fraiche melt in, then bring to a gentle simmer and stir in the dijon and baby spinach.

Taste for seasoning, then squeeze in the lemon juice and serve up with the green beans.

Sweet Treats

Chocolate mousse

* *Makes 4*
* *Longer recipe*
* *Make ahead*

200g dark chocolate
4 eggs
1 large scoop (45g) vanilla protein powder

Break the chocolate into a bowl. Fill a small pan of water about a quarter of the way up. Make sure to pick a pan that the bowl of chocolate fits snugly onto. Put the water on to heat, and when it boils, nestle the bowl on the pan, reduce the heat and leave the chocolate to melt – it should take 6–8 minutes. When melted, turn off the heat and leave while you carry on with the rest of the recipe.

Separate the eggs into two large bowls.

Add the protein powder and about 50ml water to the egg yolks and whisk until the mix becomes a smooth, thick liquid – the consistency of very thick double cream.

Using a clean whisk, whisk up the egg whites until they have ballooned in volume and hold their own weight.

Beat the slightly cooled, melted chocolate into the egg yolk mixture, then tip a third of the egg whites into the same mix and beat in.

Stir the remaining two-thirds of the egg whites through the chocolate mix using a folding, slicing motion.

When all of the whites are well incorporated, divide the mixture between four small glasses and leave to cool and set. The mousses will be ready after about 2 hours.

Baked maple apples

3 small or 2 large eating apples,
cut in half
70g softened butter
25ml maple syrup
1 tsp vanilla extract
½ tsp ground cinnamon
40g raisins

To serve
3 tbsp crème fraiche
30g walnuts, roughly chopped

Preheat the oven to 190°C (fan 170°C/gas mark 5).

Take each apple half, and using a teaspoon, scoop the seeded core out of the apple half and discard. Line the apple halves up in a small roasting tray and slide into the hot oven. Bake the halves for 10 minutes.

While the apples are baking, beat together the butter, maple syrup, vanilla, cinnamon and raisins.

After 10 minutes, remove the apples from the oven and roughly dot and splodge the butter mixture as evenly as possible over the top before returning the apples to the hot oven. Bake for a further 15 minutes.

Remove the apples from the oven. They should be cooked through. (If you like them very soft, then cook on for longer, but cover them to stop the raisins burning.)

Plate the apples up, drop on a little crème fraiche and sprinkle over the chopped walnuts.

BLACKCURRANT
poached pears

* Serves 4
* Make ahead

4 pears, peeled
250ml Ribena
2 star anise
1 large cinnamon stick
1 vanilla pod, seeds scraped
from the inside and reserved
4 tbsp mascarpone
chopped pecans, to serve

Lay the pears in a saucepan that's just big enough to tightly hold them in one layer. Pour over the Ribena, then add just enough water to cover the pears. Add the star anise, cinnamon and vanilla seeds.

Bring slowly to the boil, then reduce the heat and simmer very gently for about 15 minutes, or until a butter knife pushes through the flesh of the pear. When you're happy the pears are cooked, fish them gently out of the liquid onto a dish, then pour over all but about a third of the liquid.

Put the remaining poaching liquid back onto the heat and bring to the boil. Reduce by a third.

When you're ready to serve, lay the pears in bowls and spoon over some of the reduced liquid. Dollop a spoonful of mascarpone onto each plate and finish with a scattering of chopped pecans.

Coconut macaroons

* Makes 6
* Make ahead

2 eggs, whites only
20g caster sugar
1 large scoop (45g) vanilla
protein powder
100g desiccated coconut
50g dark chocolate, melted

Preheat the oven to 160°C (fan 140°C/gas mark 3), and line a flat baking tray with non-stick baking parchment.

Place the egg whites in a large, clean mixing bowl and whisk with an electric hand whisk until the whites are frothy and hold their own weight. Spoon in the sugar a little at a time while continuing to whisk the whites.

When the sugar has all been incorporated, slowly add the protein powder to the egg mix, continuing to mix as you sprinkle it in.

When all the sugar and protein powder has been incorporated, the whites should be glossy and thick. Fold the coconut into the mix, then, using two spoons, dollop six large mounds onto the lined baking tray.

Slide the tray into the oven and bake for 8 minutes.

Remove the macaroons from the oven and let them cool a little, then drizzle the melted chocolate all over. Eat warm or leave to cool to room temperature.

Mango & mint fools

* Serves 4
* Make ahead

2 ripe mangoes, flesh only
(390g)
30g icing sugar
1 scoop (30g) vanilla protein
powder
275ml double cream
mint leaves, to serve – optional

Roughly chop up three-quarters of the mango flesh and place in a blender. Roughly dice the rest of the mango and reserve for later.

Add the icing sugar and protein powder to the mango and blitz until smooth. Tip the mango puree into a bowl and fold the remaining diced mango through.

Whisk up the double cream until it just holds its own weight, then gently fold into the mango puree, just rippling the two components rather than completely mixing them together.

Carefully dollop the mixture into four glasses, then place in the fridge to cool down for an hour. Just before serving, garnish with mint leaves.

Mini strawb pavlovas

* Makes 6
* Longer recipe

4 eggs, whites only
200g caster sugar
½ tsp white wine vinegar
1 tsp cornflour
400g strawberries, stalk removed and berry cut into thin slices (pound-coin thickness)
juice of ½ lemon
3 tsp icing sugar
400ml double cream
3 digestive biscuits

Preheat the oven to 180°C (fan 160°C/gas mark 4).

Place the egg whites in a large clean bowl and whisk well until light and fluffy and able to hold their own weight. Add 1 tablespoon of sugar and whisk for about 30 seconds before adding another. Continue this process, ensuring you don't add more than 1 tablespoon of sugar at a time, and giving the mix a good whisk until all the sugar is used up and the egg whites are very stiff and glossy.

Add the white wine vinegar and the cornflour and whisk again. Continue to whisk for a good 2–3 minutes to be sure that all the ingredients are absolutely mixed together.

When you are happy with the mix, dollop six large mounds of meringue onto a flat baking tray lined with non-stick baking parchment. Using the back of a spoon, push the centre of each mound down a little to create a nest shape.

Slide the nests into the oven and immediately reduce the heat to 100°C (fan 80°C/gas mark ¼). Leave the nests to cook like this for 30 minutes, then turn the oven off and leave to cool.

Meanwhile, mix the strawberries and lemon juice in a bowl, then sieve over the icing sugar. Leave to sit until you're ready to eat.

Just before serving, whisk up the double cream until it's just thick enough to hold its own weight.

Carefully sit the mini pavlovas on a serving plate, dollop on some double cream and top with the strawberries. Crumble over the digestive biscuits and serve immediately.

Use a clean mixing bowl to whisk up the eggs and sugar and don't rush when spooning in the sugar.

Watermelon jelly

* Serves 6
* Longer recipe
* Make ahead

1 medium watermelon, flesh only (780g)
200g strawberries, stalks removed and strawberries cut roughly, plus extra to decorate
15 sheets of gelatine
120g sugar

The day before you wish to serve, place the watermelon flesh and chopped strawberries into a food processor and blitz until smooth. Pass the blitzed mix through a sieve, discarding the bits of flesh left behind in the sieve as you go. You should end up with about 1.2 litres of fruit juice.

Submerge the gelatine leaves in cold water and leave to soak for about 5 minutes, or until softened.

Pour about one third of the watermelon and strawberry juice into a saucepan and add the sugar. Turn the heat on under the pan and heat gently, stirring to allow the sugar to dissolve.

Do not let the juice boil, but bring it up to a simmer, then turn off the heat.

Pick out some of the soaked gelatine leaves and give them a good squeeze. Gently lower the leaves into the warm liquid, stirring as they go in. The gelatine will dissolve in the warm liquid. Repeat the process with the remaining leaves.

When all the gelatine has been incorporated into the liquid, stir it back into the main batch of watermelon and strawberry juice. Pour the mix into a large jelly mould, then place in the fridge overnight.

When you're ready to eat, gently warm the jelly mould in warm water, then place a plate on top and flip the whole lot over. The jelly should drop neatly from the mould.

Index

Thank yous

I can't believe I'm writing the acknowledgements for my 6th book already. I want to start by saying a big thank you to my publisher Carole from Bluebird for continuing to help me create beautiful books that I'm really proud of. I've had the same awesome team work on all of my books and I'm really lucky to have Maja and Bianca helping to bring my recipes to life. I absolutely love the photography in this book and I hope you enjoy it too.

Thank you to all of my team including Bev, Megan, Martha and Hockley for all your help and support with this book.

To the Love of my life Rosie. Thank you for bringing me so much happiness and for carrying our first baby into the world this year.

Big up all my besties Nikki, Oscar, George, Luca, Ted, Keads, Justin, Brendon, Gilbert, Seymour, Jonny Martin, and Kleatus. I can't wait to make more memories together.

Finally thank you to everyone who follows me on social media, cooks my recipes and does my workouts. You are my inspiration to keep working hard.

Love, Joe

Want to see more recipes and transform your body? Check out my other life-changing books …

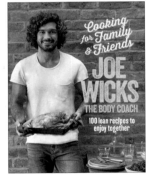

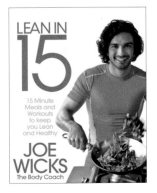

First published 2018 by Bluebird
This omnibus edition first published 2019 by Bluebird
an imprint of Pan Macmillan
The Smithson, 6 Briset Street, London EC1M 5NR
Associated companies throughout the world
www.panmacmillan.com

ISBN 978-1-5290-3634-3

9 8 7 6 5 4 3 2 1

A CIP catalogue record for this book is available from the British Library.

Printed and bound in China.

Publisher **Carole Tonkinson**
Senior Editor **Martha Burley**
Assistant Editor **Hockley Raven Spare**
Senior Production Controller **Ena Matagic**
Art Direction & Design **Jilly Topping**
Prop Styling **Lydia Brun**
Food Styling **Bianca Nice, Sunil Vijayakar, Lizzie Harris**

With thanks to Labour and Wait for loaning products for the photography. Visit the website at www.labourandwait.co.uk

Visit **www.panmacmillan.com** to read more about all our books and to buy them. You will also find features, author interviews and news of any author events, and you can sign up for e-newsletters so that you're always first to hear about our new releases.